The Leavenworth Schools and the Old Army

Contributions in Military History
Series Editors: THOMAS E. GRIESS and JAY LUVAAS

The River and the Rock: The History of Fortress West Point, 1775-1783
DAVE R. PALMER

Dear Miss Em: General Eichelberger's War in the Pacific, 1942-1945
JAY LUVAAS, editor

Schoolbooks and Krags: The United States Army in the Pacific, 1898-1902
JOHN M. GATES

American Gunboat Diplomacy and the Old Navy, 1877-1889
KENNETH J. HAGAN

The Image of the Army Officer in America: Background for Current Views
C. ROBERT KEMBLE

The Memoirs of Henry Heth
HENRY HETH, edited by JAMES L. MORRISON, JR.

Against the Specter of a Dragon: The Campaign for American Military Preparedness, 1914-1917
JOHN P. FINNEGAN

The Way of the Fox: American Strategy in the War for America, 1775-1783
DAVE R. PALMER

History of the Art of War: Within the Framework of Political History
HANS DELBRÜCK, translated by WALTER J. RENFROE, JR.

The General: Robert L. Bullard and Officership in the United States Army, 1881-1925
ALLAN R. MILLETT

The Twenty-First Missouri: From Home Guard to Union Regiment
LESLIE ANDERS

The Politics of the Second Front: American Military Planning and Diplomacy in Coalition Warfare, 1941-1943
MARK A. STOLER

The Anatomy of a Small War: The Soviet-Japanese Struggle for Changkufeng/ Khasan, 1938
ALVIN D. COOX

Reconsiderations on the Revolutionary War: Selected Essays
DON HIGGINBOTHAM, editor

Timothy K. Nenninger   # THE
LEAVENWORTH SCHOOLS
AND THE OLD ARMY

Education, Professionalism, and
the Officer Corps of the
United States Army,
1881-1918

Contributions in Military History, Number 15

GREENWOOD PRESS
Westport, Connecticut • London, England

Library of Congress Cataloging in Publication Data

Nenninger, Timothy K
 The Leavenworth schools and the old Army.

 (Contributions in military history ; no. 15
ISSN 0084-9251)
 Bibliography: p.
 Includes index.
 1. United States. Army Service Schools, Fort
Leavenworth, Kan.—History. 2. Military education—
United States—History. 3. United States. Army—
Officers—History. I. Title. II. Series: Contributions
in military history ; no. 15.
U415.N46   355'.07'1178138   77-91105
ISBN 0-313-20047-5

Library of Congress Catalog Card Number: 77-91105
ISBN: 0-313-20047-5
ISSN: 0084-9251

First published in 1978

Greenwood Press, Inc.
51 Riverside Avenue, Westport, Connecticut 06880

Printed in the United States of America

10 9 8 7 6 5 4 3 2 1

For my mother
and father

CONTENTS

Acknowledgments   ix

1 Professionalism, Education, and the Art of War
       in the Nineteenth Century   3

2 General Sherman and the School
       of Application   21

3 The Era of Wagner and Swift   34

4 Leavenworth and the Elihu Root Reforms   53

5 General Bell and the New Leavenworth   68

6 Line School, Staff College, and Leavenworth
       Doctrine   82

7 The Schools and the Army   112

8 The American Expeditionary Forces
       Experience   134

Appendixes   155

Bibliographical Essay   163

Index   169

ACKNOWLEDGMENTS

Of the several archivists and librarians who assisted me in the research for this study, two deserve special mention. The late Mary Johnson and William H. Cunliffe, both of the National Archives, greatly facilitated my early gropings in the voluminous records relating to Leavenworth and the Old Army. A number of my colleagues generously shared their research with me, including Professor Allan R. Millett of Ohio State University, Dr. Forrest C. Pogue of the Smithsonian Institution, and Dr. Edgar F. Raines, Jr., of Silver Lake College.

Throughout the period of my research and writing, Professor Edward M. Coffman of the University of Wisconsin gave sound advice, provided fruitful research leads, and offered constructive criticism; I am grateful for all three. I would like also to thank the series editors, Colonel Thomas E. Griess and Professor Jay Luvaas, who suggested several revisions in my manuscript. Professor Coffman, Mr. Cunliffe, Dr. John Greenwood of the Office of Air Force History, Colonel Alfred E. Hurley of the U. S. Air Force Academy, Thomas E. Kelly III of the Center of Military History, and Professor Donald W. Smythe of John Carroll University read portions of my manuscript. I appreciated their useful comments on style, content, and interpretation. The sole responsibility for this work is mine, of course. Finally I would like to thank my wife, Ina, for her encouragement and assistance during the several years I have worked on this project.

The Leavenworth Schools and the Old Army

1

PROFESSIONALISM, EDUCATION, AND THE ART OF WAR IN THE NINETEENTH CENTURY

To cope with the technological, organizational, and tactical changes occurring in warfare during the late nineteenth and early twentieth centuries, the United States Army needed educated, well-trained, professional officers. Thus in 1881 the War Department established the School of Application for Calvary and Infantry at Fort Leavenworth, Kansas, as a training school for officers.

The School of Application, first in a series of variously named schools at Fort Leavenworth, continued until the Spanish-American War to train junior officers in professional military subjects, particularly small-unit tactics. Before 1898 the institution gradually improved as the course of study became more sophisticated. For two years following the Spanish War, Leavenworth reverted to its original role of teaching small-unit tactics and company administration to young, largely untrained lieutenants. Between 1904 and 1916, when the two principal schools were the Army School of the Line and the Army Staff College, Leavenworth became a postgraduate military institution that prepared well-qualified officers for general staff duties and positions of high command. Although the curriculum included mili-

tary engineering, law, and foreign languages, the emphasis was
on military art, which encompassed tactics, strategy, logistics,
and military history. As Leavenworth developed and maintained
professional standards and added to the knowledge of the officer
corps, its importance to the army grew.

Continuing changes in warfare, as well as pressures from within the service, forced changes in the organization, curriculum,
and selection procedures for students and instructors. Ideas
from foreign armies, particularly the German, personal experiences, and standing American military doctrine guided War
Department officials and Leavenworth instructors in setting the
objectives of the schools, determining the curriculum, and implementing the program of instruction. A number of people in
both the War Department and at Leavenworth were leading
influences in the development of the institution: William T.
Sherman in establishing the School of Application; Arthur L.
Wagner and Eben Swift in creating a distinctive Leavenworth
doctrine and self-image, Elihu Root and J. Franklin Bell in determining the role and organization of the school in the early
twentieth century, and John F. Morrison in formulating curriculum to meet that role.

Leavenworth was not the only institution concerned with
achieving army reform through military education. But because
most of its graduates exhibited a strong sense of professionalism,
praised the schools, and attempted to apply what they learned
there to their subsequent duties, gradually the rest of the service
accepted the doctrines and techniques taught at Leavenworth.
This trend was most pronounced when graduates rose to positions of authority. Because the number of graduates was small
and they held relatively low rank and because some senior officers were skeptical of the expertise of school-trained officers,
Leavenworth had a limited impact on the army before 1917.
In World War I, however, Leavenworth graduates made a significant contribution to the conduct of American operations,
especially in the American Expeditionary Forces. The AEF
experience culminated the previous forty years of development
and ensured the schools of a significant future role in army
education.

In the course of these forty years Leavenworth went far toward achieving the objective of professional education: "to inculcate the corpus of knowledge, the complement of skills, and the traits of personality and character which contribute the distinctive features of a particular craft."[1] More than the other postgraduate military schools, Leavenworth had an impact on the developing professionalism of individual officers and on the army. In common with European staff colleges of the era, the scope of instruction at Leavenworth remained limited to the conduct of war itself—to armies and battles. Concern by the military with a wide range of economic, social, diplomatic, and political questions did not come, either in the United States or Europe, until World War I, and military education did not reflect such concerns until after the war. By 1916 Leavenworth did produce competent commanders and staff officers able to analyze complex problems and understand the techniques of high command and general staff work.[2]

Today the Command and General Staff College remains "the source and fount of doctrines and procedures" for the army. When John W. Masland and Laurence I. Radway studied the army's educational system during the 1950s, they found many officers who questioned the value of the senior joint and service colleges but none who questioned that of Leavenworth. By then Leavenworth had become the most important educational experience in an officer's career.[3] Leavenworth was not always that important, however. Between 1881 and World War I, its reputation continually grew, it began teaching what today has become established army doctrine, and it made a major contribution to the professionalization of the officer corps.

One scholar defines a profession as a "peculiar type of functional group with highly specialized characteristics": its corporateness, sense of responsibility, and expertise. Members of a profession share a sense of unity and consciousness of themselves as a group apart from all others. The sense of corporateness results from the shared discipline and training necessary for professional competence, the common bond of work, and the social responsibility unique to that profession. A professional works in a social context, performing a service essential to the functioning of its client, society. Because the professional monopolizes skills necessary to perform essential functions, he has a responsibility to perform that function when required. Expertise, the third characteristic, is acquired by prolonged education and experience and is a measuring rod of professional competence. Professional expertise usually is characterized by a broad, general education followed by the acquisition of specialized, narrowly applicable skills and knowledge.[4]

An individual becomes professionalized through a wide variety of experiences. Professional socialization, the "process by which members of a profession learn the values, attitudes, and behavior deemed to be appropriate to their roles within the profession," occurs throughout an individual's career.[5] Experience, the informal social organization of the profession, and the social, economic, and educational background of the individual have an effect on professional development. Professional education is also important because it affects the development of corporateness, responsibility, and expertise. For the military profession schooling is particularly significant because of the limited opportunities officers have to practice their profession—to command and manage troops in combat. Other than war, school is among the principal means by which officers can develop professional expertise.

The American army did not suddenly become professionalized during the last two or three decades of the nineteenth century. Professionalization of the officer corps was a dynamic, continuing process whose roots lay in the period between the War of 1812 and the Civil War. It began with a group of young officers who had risen to responsible positions during the War of 1812. Their wartime experiences and career aspirations, reinforced by the American social environment, created a sense of common purpose among them, and they wanted to rationalize military administration, develop a regular officer selection process, and cultivate an intellectual, scientific approach to solving military problems. The officer corps by the 1860s had moved in the direction of centralization, uniformity, and efficient management, but it still retained individualistic, unstructured, unprofessional elements.[6]

With the exception of the service academies, all the permanent characteristics that identify the American military as a profession originated in the years between the Civil War and World War I: journals, professional associations, and, most prominently, the postgraduate schools. For the antebellum officer corps a West Point education was sufficient professional training; by the late nineteenth century additional schooling was required. Clearly the definition of a professional was changing, particularly with regard to the required expertise. Further, the self-image of American officers was reinforced during this period by an awareness of themselves as "a learned profession in the same sense as law or medicine, being consciously aware of the progress they had made in this direction."[7] Before the Civil War, officers had not regarded themselves in such strictly professional terms.

American military reform did not develop in a vacuum. The late nineteenth century saw the rise of other professions and the founding of educational institutions for these professions. Sometimes consciously, sometimes not, the military emulated the civilians; the reverse was also true. Most nations founded staff colleges before business schools, while the first schools of engineering and technology were usually military.[8] In the United States West Point, founded in 1803 as an academy for military engineers, was the first engineering college, and throughout the nineteenth century it had a number of imitators. From 1880 to World War I, however, military educators in the United States certainly learned more from their civilian counterparts than the civilians learned from the military.

Particularly after Leavenworth reopened following the Spanish-American War, those shaping the school's policy were vaguely aware of the changes that had been occurring in American higher education for the previous twenty years. A number of instructors, for instance, belonged to the American Historical Association, attended its annual meetings, and participated in its programs. Other instructors had been professors of military science and tactics at civilian universities where they had been exposed to American higher education. Occasionally civilian educators, such as University of Nebraska Professor Frederick Morrow Fling, visited Leavenworth to observe the course, analyze instructional

methods, and offer advice on improving the school. A few instructors had attended civilian schools for advanced work in
such fields as law, engineering, and history. Instructors at Leavenworth used the case method to teach law and applied techniques
common to graduate history courses to instruction at the
schools.

The reformers at Leavenworth, as well as the other military
progressives of that era, were products of their time. They were
aware of the general trends in American university education
and applied instructional techniques common to the civilian
equivalents of Leavenworth. Similarly the turn-of-the-century
attempt to reform military management and control, exemplified
by the Elihu Root reforms, can be viewed in terms of contemporary thinking of the Progressive era about administration and
organization. Among others Russell F. Weigley has noted the
parallel development during the Progressive era of the civilian
and military sectors from invertebrate to vertebrate societies.
Economic institutions and government bureaucracies, as well
as the army, attempted to create a "national skeletal structure"
to give order, leadership, and direction to their organizations.
The parallels were not exact; the army already had the outlines
of a nationwide hierarchy, and the officer corps had a cohesion
not often found among civilian professions of the period. Yet
there were similarities in the scientific management techniques
employment by both and in the socioeconomic background of
business, political, and military leaders. In addition, after 1898
these leaders developed a commonality of interest in reforming
their respective institutions to deal more effectively with America's expanded overseas acquisitions.[9]

Despite these similarities among American civilian and military educators and reformers, more often the impetus for reform
arose out of conditions unique to the army. Although civilian
secretaries of war, such as Redfield Proctor (1889-91) and Elihu
Root (1899-1904), led reform, the ideas and essential details on
which the various reforms rested came from the professional
officer corps. Often reform measures had been debated for years
in the service journals. Frequently the ideas had come from
foreign military sources. Foreign influence was pervasive in the

establishment, evolution, organization, and instruction of the Leavenworth schools. While between 1881 and 1917 Leavenworth grew in an atmosphere of progressivism and paralleled the growth of American higher education, its roots, instruction techniques, and, to a limited extent, doctrine, were European.

Military history has often been international history; national armies have fought against each other, fought as allies, or studied and imitated one another. Armies studied other armies as potential enemies but also to keep abreast of changing tactics, weapons, and organization. As technological and organizational improvements brought about a revolution in the art of war during the nineteenth century, observation of foreign armies became a necessity. Military attachés and neutral military observers who accompanied belligerent armies were an accepted part of the military scene and the conduit through which the latest information passed. The accumulation of information was merely the initial step. How or whether an army used the information—to prepare war plans, design uniforms and equipment, or modify weapons and tactics—was more crucial. Because armies usually reflected the society from which they emerged and were the products of deep tradition, few could unabashedly imitate other armies. Neither could they afford to ignore the changes in organization, tactics, and weapons manifest in the mid-century wars.[10] (See appendix 1.)

Extensive building of transportation networks, including macadamized highways, canals, and railways, accelerated movement and permitted easier and longer-range supply of armies. The emergence of a cartographic science made practical for the first time extensive and detailed maps, a necessity for planning military operations. The most important element was the changed conditions on the field of battle that began in the seventeenth century with the introduction of the flintlock musket, socket bayonet, and mobile field artillery. Rifled weapons reinforced this process by which infantry remained largely invulnerable to cavalry, increased its rate and accuracy of fire, and improved its maneuverability. As firepower and mobility increased, tactical formations became more dispersed. An army in the field, in battle and on the march, was no longer a single

body but a group of miniature armies, able to move simulta-
neously on parallel roads, which seldom came together under
the eye of the commander. War had become "an art to be pursued upon the map, and with an immensely greater number of
permutations and combinations possible than ever before."[11]
As it became more complicated, the conduct of war required of
its practitioners more intelligence, knowledge, skill, and preparation.

The commander needed information from and about his
widely dispersed troops. In the past acquisition of the requisite
information had been simple because all the troops were within
direct view. Written reports by subordinate commanders and
staff officers were now the source of information. Written rather
than verbal orders were a necessity. Because of the dispersal of
forces, maps assumed even greater importance. Preparation of
war plans to guide initial operational phases of a war and preparation of staff officers and commanders in postgraduate military schools became a peacetime necessity. All of the major
European powers formulated mobilization plans and created
staff colleges or war colleges. Because in the late nineteenth century the United States faced no immediate military threat, the
war plans of the Europeans and the process of preparing such
plans was of only limited interest to the Americans. Senior
European military schools, on the other hand, were of great
interest.

The development of the military as a profession closely paral-
led the development of military schools. In Europe as feudal
institutions broke down, military leadership became less the
prerogative of the landed aristocracy. Intellect, expertise, and
an understanding of the increasingly technical aspects of war
replaced "character," which the aristocracy believed only it
possessed, as the criteria for military leadership. "Character"
gave the postfeudal officer corps of such nations as Prussia,
France, and England the homogeneity necessary for cohesion
and understanding in times of stress. In the industrial age of
the nineteenth century, this conception of the officer as heroic
leader began to change, although vestiges of it still remain. The
increasingly complex, technological nature of war, the growing

specialization and division of labor in all aspects of society, and the rise of democratic ideals and consequential decline of the aristocracy led to another view of the officer—that of the military manager. The skills required for such a role were not genetic traits common only to the aristocracy but could be acquired through experience and by means of professional education. Within this conception of the professional officer, two contrasting ideas about military education were apparent. The first was that officers could be molded from an early age by rigid schooling, with much emphasis on mathematics to discipline the mind and drill to instill physical discipline. The second view was that officers could be trained, after they had first acquired a basic civilian type education, by a program of practical instruction in professional military subjects. In Europe during the nineteenth century, these developments accompanied the establishment of the staff colleges, which buttressed the technical, narrow education officers earlier had received only in the cadet schools.[12]

The three principal European staff colleges had been established in the aftermath of national military calamities. Gerhard von Scharnhorst opened the *Kriegsakademie* in 1810 as part of the general Prussian military reforms in the wake of Jena. The British Staff College opened in 1858, the product of a wave of interest in military reform, particularly in improving the education of officers, following the debacle in the Crimea. In 1878 the *Ecole supérieure de guerre* began under Jules Louis Lewal, its first commandant, in reaction to poor French preparations for the war against the Prussians in 1870. Indeed its goal of preparing students for staff and command work was pursued largely by a minute study of French mistakes in that previous war.[13] Leavenworth evolved from quite different circumstances and remained unique from these European institutions. Yet military educators in Europe and America faced some of the same problems and reached similar solutions.

The question of how much general education, especially remedial work, to present at the expense of military courses perplexed instructors at both the *Kriegsakademie* between 1810 and 1825 and at Leavenworth between 1881 and 1890. Pedagogy also concerned both. Before 1820 Carl von Clausewitz, the most famous of the early instructors at the Prussian academy, wanted to adapt the applicatory method whereby students became active participants in their education rather than passive listeners. The school did not become the activist, professional school he envisaged until the 1860s.[14] Leavenworth in the 1880s faced educational issues quite similar to those encountered by the Germans sixty years earlier.

After 1870 the *Kriegsakademie* had changed considerably from the time of Clausewitz. The three-year course then included nonprofessional subjects like history, geography, science, and foreign languages. Because the intent of the course was to produce operational staff officers and commanders, applied tactics and military history consumed most instruction time. Through the applicatory method, the academy endeavored to familiarize students with "the endless diversity of the conditions of modern battle" and prepare them to cope with that diversity even under stress.[15] Instruction concentrated on staff techniques and procedures, especially with regard to the conduct of large-scale operations, which the General Staff considered its special preserve. One graduate appraised the result: "The exercises at the Military Academy were most interesting, at times absolutely fascinating, but did not concern themselves in the least with the technique of the conduct of battles. No order that would have been given in combat was ever discussed. . . ; it all turned around the operational element, around the question of whether to move forwards or backwards, or to the side, whether to envelope right or left."[16] *Kriegsakademie* graduates tended to be competent operations officers who sometimes had a far too narrow focus and a far too limited concept of the conduct of war.

By the end of the nineteenth century, the *Kriegsakademie* had become the crucial element in the system whereby the German Army selected its most promising young officers, provided intensive academic and practical training, offered accelerated promotions and choice assignments for the best of an already select group, rotated officers between staff and line, and finally placed the most outstanding officers in General Staff positions or important field commands. The system stimulated an exceptional esprit de corps and a homogeneity of outlook, and it gave great status and prestige to the General Staff throughout the German Army.

For many years Camberley, the British Staff College, lacked such an intimate relationship with a functioning general staff; indeed there was no Imperial General Staff until 1904. Because this was similar to the American experience, between 1858 and 1914 Camberley's development was remarkably similar to the evolution of Leavenworth from 1881 to 1916. Over time the curriculum at both schools changed from an unsophisticated lecture and recitation course in basic military skills for subalterns to an advanced course in staff and command procedures for specially qualified company and field grade officers. For both schools significant changes, from a course stressing absorption of knowledge to one focusing on learning by doing, occurred in the 1890s. At Camberley G. F. R. Henderson and H. J. T. Hildyard made the critical analysis of military history and the solution of tactical problems the core of the course. Just as Leavenworth improved dramatically after the Spanish-American War, so did the British Staff College after the South African War. The Staff College acquired a distinct sense of purpose with the creation of the Imperial General Staff, as Camberley became the principal supplier of general staff officers and a center for the promulgation of an anti-German, pro-French continental strategy.[17] The development of a distinctive strategic doctrine was the only major characteristic Leavenworth did not share with Camberley. The similarities were instructive of how two armies responded similarly to changes in the nature of warfare despite differences in their strategic and military positions. It further suggested that perhaps universal, international influences had more impact on military development than did internal pressures.

American army officers of the later nineteenth century, generally considered to be progressive or reform minded, were often those most aware of European armies, wars, and military schools. Officers involved in the development of Leavenworth pointed to the Europeans, especially the Germans, for justification of advanced military education, for methods of instruction, and for books to use in the curriculum. Some regarded the Prussians

as the ultimate professionals, the ideal to be emulated. Others
acknowledged that specific foreign ideas or institutions were
applicable in the United States Army but cautioned against
uncritically accepting these into the American setting with its
unique tradition, legal system, and heterogeneous population.
Nonetheless between 1880 and 1916 foreign military developments very much influenced how Leavenworth evolved.

Jurgen Herbst, a historian of education, has written of the
"transfer of culture" that occurred when American graduate
students studied history, economics, sociology, and political
science in German universities and returned to the United
States where many became leaders in the rise of the American
university. The transfer of culture was not without problems.
As Herbst summarized: "In any society, culture may be said
to consist of the interaction of its institutions and ideas. Thus
the American who went to German universities to acquire the
tools of scholarship brought home not only tools but ideas
as well. When the ideas proved difficult to assimilate to American conditions, the scholars sought to modify or discard them,
only to realize that their scholarly equipment, torn from its
ideological setting, would no longer serve until a new context
of ideas could be developed."[18] The attempt to adapt foreign
military ideas and aspects of foreign military institutions to
Leavenworth had a number of parallels with the process Herbst
described.

The first-rate, specialized scientific and scholarly training
drew American students to the German universities. American
officers saw the German Army as the most successful, modern
military force then in existence. Both groups wanted to increase
the professionalization of their respective fields. In addition the
scholars stressed academic freedom while the soldiers hoped to
promote a more analytical attitude among the officer corps.
Rigorous training to produce disciplined minds was another con-
comitant goal of both. For soldiers as well as scholars, the adap-
tion of methodology and institutions was far more successful
than that of ideas. Graduate departments in history and political
science, research seminars, scholarly associations, and scholarly
publications were all products of the German historical school.

But the German-trained scholars were unable to impose their
pattern of political and institutional development on history as
taught in early twentieth-century America. They mixed German
ideas with American facts and consequently foundered on the
shoals of cultural diversity.[19] Similarly, features of the applicatory
method of tactical instruction, adapted from the Germans by
Leavenworth instructors, remain part of current American military instructional doctrine. On the other hand, Leavenworth
instructors rejected many aspects of German tactics, while the
relationship among the Prussian emperor, the war minister, and
the chief of the Imperial General Staff could never have been
duplicated by the American president, secretary of war, and
chief of the War Department General Staff.

There were several steps in the process by which Leavenworth
assimilated foreign military thought. Some observers, including
Emory Upton and William Ludlow, had reported on the postgraduate military schools in Europe and recommended that the
American army establish similar institutions. Receptive War
Department officials, recognizing the advantages of such schools
and the needs of the United States Army, established the schools
as reflections of the European institutions. At a more practical
level, Leavenworth instructors like Arthur L. Wagner wrote
books comparing the military experience of the American Civil
War with the German wars of unification. Eben Swift adapted
German methodology to the American situation, introducing
the applicatory method of tactical instruction at Leavenworth.
Particularly after Leavenworth reopened following the Spanish-
American War, the curriculum included translations of German
textbooks on tactics (Balck), strategy (von der Goltz), and organization (von Schellendorff). But gradually instructors at the
schools prepared their own texts, which replaced the foreign
works. The lasting foreign legacy to Leavenworth was more in
the area of methodology (the applicatory method) than ideas
(tactical doctrine).

Factors unique to the American army also influenced the
dynamics of military reform and the evolution of military education. Historians have characterized the late nineteenth century
as the "dark ages" and "the twilight" of the United States

Army.[20] It was a period of stagnation but also a time of transition. The end of the Civil War brought rapid demobilization and retrenchment. Congress and the rest of the country ignored the military except in time of Indian uprisings and labor disturbances. With the gradual cessation of the Indian wars in the 1880s, the one active mission of the army disappeared. Although a few officers, and an occasional civilian, began to reassess the military's role in national policy and to consider how the army should be structured to meet that role, the task of the reformers was difficult.

Scattered in small garrisons in the West, the army after the Civil War succumbed to a "post psychology." For too many officers the petty details of routine garrison administration were the limit of their professional concern. Field service, not the systematic study of past campaigns or the theoretical analysis of the art of war, provided the sole opportunity for an officer to learn about tactics and strategy. Service against Indians required little knowledge of what officers at the time called "civilized warfare." Officers gained expertise in Indian fighting by fighting, not by reading books on the subject. The immediate needs of the army required officers to possess little more than common sense and the most basic understanding of weapons and tactics. Often the older officers discouraged study; they thought that fighting in a war (as they had) was the only way to learn soldiering. An awareness of current military problems, necessary for a change in attitudes among the officer corps and ultimately for internal reform, was slow to come.[21]

The absence of any immediate threat to the security of the United States encouraged apathy toward the military. The army seemed to possess the capability to deal with the Indians and to control labor disturbances and the soldiers realized there was little threat of war with European countries. Phillip Sheridan, the commanding general, wrote in his 1884 annual report: "Excepting for our ocean commerce and for our seaboard cities, I do not think we should be much alarmed about probability of wars with foreign powers."[22]

Lessons from the Civil War and Europe, however, argued powerfully for reform. The Union Army succeeded in the Civil

War and the Regulars did good work in the West in spite of, not because of, the American military system. The Regulars were competent campaigners but were short of men, often had unsatisfactory equipment, and lacked any provision for their expansion in time of a major war. Technology, the industrial revolution, and changes in military organization, evident in the midcentury wars, provided lessons for those willing and able to think about the military system of this era.

Emory Upton was among those who tried to come to grips with the changing nature of war and adjust the United States Army to the changes. A West Point graduate, Civil War hero, major general at twenty-five, commandant of the Artillery School at Fort Monroe, and protégé of William T. Sherman (the commanding general from 1869 to 1883), he became the principal writer and thinker on military reform of the late nineteenth century. Based on his study of European and Asian armies and the previous century of American experience, Upton proposed changes ranging from regimental organization to the national system of mobilizing reserves. Periodic military schooling for enlisted men, junior officers, and experienced commanders was essential to the other reforms Upton advocated. His own experience at West Point and the Artillery School and his perception of the impact of the *Kriegsakademie* on the German Army convinced Upton of that. By emphasizing the role of the Regular Army over that of citizen soldiers, principally the militia, he developed a following among the officer corps, especially the progressive minded who wrote for and read the professional journals.[23]

During the last two decades of the nineteenth century, officers filled the service journals and popular periodicals with articles advocating Uptonian reforms. With the rising sentiment for American expansion in the 1890s and a widened definition of national security, the reformers attempted to bring their proposals in line with the changing diplomatic realities. Growing overseas interests gave their arguments added impetus.

Several administrative reforms had strengthened the army by the end of the century. Gradually the War Department abandoned some of the small frontier posts and concentrated troops in larger, regimental-size garrisons, reducing hardships and operating expenses and furthering esprit de corps and training. Congress appropriated money to strengthen coast defenses, although it did not spend nearly as much as most officers wanted. The reformers made their greatest progress in improving the quality of the officer corps in 1878 when Congress limited commissions to West Point graduates and civilians who passed a rigorous examination and four years later established sixty-four as the mandatory retirement age. Although these reforms improved internal efficiency, their impact was limited: they did not change the American military system or how officers thought about their profession.[24]

As the Europeans had shown, improvements in the educational system of an army could change how officers thought about their profession and thus help stimulate and perpetuate other reforms. Upton and other army reformers recognized that unless the American army adopted some system of postgraduate military education, there was little sense in attempting to emulate other progressive aspects of foreign armies.

By 1880 the need for postgraduate military education was obvious. The experience in Europe and the demands of the military profession in the United States required it. The question was no longer academic but bureaucratic. When, how, and in what form would the American army undertake a systematic education of its officers?

NOTES

1. William E. Simons, *Liberal Education in the Service Academies* (New York: Bureau of Publications, Teachers College of Columbia University, 1965), p. 6; also see William J. McGlothlin, *Patterns of Professional Education* (New York: G.P. Putnam's Sons, 1960), pp. 6-7.

2. Correlli Barnett, "The Education of Military Elites," in Walter Laqueur and George L. Mosse, eds., *Education and Social Structure in the Twentieth Century* (New York: Harper & Row, 1967), pp. 209-11.

3. John W. Masland and Laurence I. Radway, *Soldiers and Scholars: Military Education and National Policy* (Princeton, N. J.: Princeton University Press, 1957), pp. 280, 300.

4. Samuel P. Huntington, *The Soldier and the State* (Cambridge, Mass.: Harvard University Press, 1957), pp. 8-10.

5. John P. Lovell, "The Cadet Phase of Professional Socialization of the West Pointer" (Ph.D. diss., University of Wisconsin, 1962), p. ii.

6. William B. Skelton, "Professionalization in the U. S. Army Officer Corps during the Age of Jackson," *Armed Forces and Society* (August 1975): 443-71.

7. Huntington, *Soldier and the State*, p. 256.

8. Barnett, "Education of Military Elites," p. 15.

9. Russell F. Weigley, "The Elihu Root Reforms and the Progressive Era," in William E. Geffen, ed., *Command and Commanders in Modern Warfare: Proceedings of the Second Military History Symposium, U. S. Air Force Academy* (Washington, D. C.: GPO, 1969), pp. 11-27; Louis Morton, "Commentary on Weigley's Paper," ibid., pp. 28-34.

10. Alfred Vagts, *The Military Attaché* (Princeton, N.J.: Princeton University Press, 1967), describes the role and the rise of attachés in the nineteenth century. Jay Luvaas, *The Military Legacy of the Civil War: The European Inheritance* (Chicago: University of Chicago Press, 1959), describes how English, German, and French officers observed both sides in the American Civil War and analyzes the impact the war had on European armies for the next fifty years. See appendix 1 for foreign observations on Leavenworth.

11. Dallas D. Irvine, "The Origin of Capital Staffs," *Journal of Modern History* 10 (June 1938): 171-74.

12. Barnett, "Education of Military Elites," pp. 193-214; Huntington, *Soldier and the State*, pp. 321-35; and Brian Bond, *The Victorian Army and the Staff College, 1854-1914* (London: Eyre Methuen, 1972), pp. 7-45, esp. p. 18.

13. Barnett, "Education of Military Elites," pp. 207-10.

14. Peter Paret, *Clausewitz and the State* (New York: Oxford University Press, 1976), pp. 272-78.

15. *Kriegsakademie* "Order of Service" and "Order of Teaching" quoted in Spenser Wilkinson, *The Brain of an Army* (London: Macmillan, 1890), pp. 80, 87.

16. Herbert Rosinski, *The German Army* (Washington, D.C.: Infantry Journal Press, 1944), p. 165.

17. Bond, *Victorian Army*, p. 326.

18. Jurgen Herbst, *The German Historical School in American Scholarship* (Ithaca, N.Y.: Cornell University Press, 1965), p. 232.

19. Ibid., pp. 124, 128.

20. William A. Ganoe, *The History of the United States Army*, rev. ed.

(Ashton, Md.: Eric Lundberg, 1964), chap. 9; Russell F. Weigley, *History of the United States Army* (New York: Macmillan, 1967), chap. 12.

21. T. Harry Williams, *Americans at War* (Baton Rouge: Louisiana State University Press, 1961), p. 87; Charles D. Rhodes, "How Best to Instruct Officers of Our Army in Tactics," *Journal of the Military Service Institution of the United States* 43 (September-October 1908): 202; James Parker, *The Old Army: Memories, 1872-1918* (Philadelphia: Dorrance and Co., 1929), p. 23.

22. Report of the Commanding General, *Annual Reports of the War Department* (Washington, D.C.: GPO, 1884), 1:48.

23. Emory Upton, *The Armies of Asia and Europe* (New York: Appleton and Co., 1878); Emory Upton, *The Military Policy of the United States* (Washington, D.C.: GPO, 1917). For works on Upton, see Stephen E. Ambrose, *Upton and the Army* (Baton Rouge: Louisiana State University Press, 1964), and Russell F. Weigley, *Towards an American Army* (New York: Columbia University Press, 1962), chaps. 7, 9.

24. The best accounts of the army reformers during this period are Graham A. Cosmas, *An Army for Empire: The United States Army in the Spanish American War* (Columbia: University of Missouri Press, 1971), chaps. 1-3; Richard Allen Andrews, "Years of Frustration: William T. Sherman, the Army, and Reform, 1869-1883" (Ph.D. diss., Northwestern University, 1968); and Weigley, *History of the U.S. Army*, chaps. 12, 13.

2

GENERAL SHERMAN
AND THE SCHOOL
OF APPLICATION

In the late 1870s several senior officers recommended establishing a school for officers at Fort Leavenworth, Kansas. The Artillery School at Fort Monroe, Virginia, reestablished in 1868 after
its demise during the Civil War, and the Engineer School of Application at Willett's Point, New York, furnished precedents.
Although these two schools provided technical training for
young artillery and engineer officers, no similar institution existed for the cavalry and infantry.

Emory Upton recommended that because of "the success
which had already attended the Artillery School . . . we should
establish schools, with similar constitution, for the infantry and
cavalry—one to be located at Atlanta, and the other at Fort
Leavenworth."[1] As early as 1877 Brigadier General John Pope,
commanding the Department of the Missouri, urged the concentration of two or three infantry regiments at Leavenworth
"for military exercises and instruction." He wanted to send
entire regiments to that post for one year to invigorate regimental discipline and esprit and to instruct officers and men in subjects with which they should be familiar but often were not
because they had no opportunity to learn while on field service.
Pope thought Leavenworth ideal for this work because of its
central location, large size, and varied terrain.[2] Although Up-

ton and Pope had different ideas about the sort of instructional
system the army needed, they agreed that something should be
done and that Fort Leavenworth was a good place for training.

As commanding general, William T. Sherman was in a position
to implement schemes of the sort Pope and Upton proposed.
More importantly he was philosophically inclined to do so.
"Uncle Billy" was a principal supporter of army reform. He
recognized the changing nature of war, the need for more thoroughly trained officers, and the advantages of military education. When Upton was commandant of the Artillery School,
Sherman encouraged him to broaden the curriculum by adding
courses in military history, strategy, and logistics.[3] Sherman
also agreed that the army needed a training center for cavalry
and infantry officers.

On May 7, 1881, Sherman ordered: "As soon as the requisite
number of troops can be assembled at Fort Leavenworth, Kansas, the commanding general Department of the Missouri will
take measures to establish a school of application for infantry
and cavalry similar to the one now in operation for the artillery
at Fortress Monroe, Virginia." Each cavalry and infantry regiment in the army would assign one lieutenant, preferably one
who had not previously received military instruction, to the
school. Sherman wanted the students to receive two years of
instruction and then rejoin their regiments, to be succeeded by
another officer from that unit "so that in time the whole Army
will thus be enabled to keep up with the rapid progress in the
science and practice of war." While at the school student officers would serve with the units assigned to the Leavenworth
garrison. By changing billets every five or six months during
the two-year course, they would learn by doing and would gain
experience in all three combat arms—artillery, cavalry, and infantry.[4]

Sherman's ideas on military education governed the establishment of the school and shaped its evolution during the first
years of its existence. Although he thought that "war is the
only real school for war," he declared that the next best way
to learn about war was at a school with the three combat arms
in one command. Sherman envisaged Leavenworth as a model

post where students carried out their duties as though at a well-regulated garrison in time of war; there would be reveille, guard mount, dress parades, retreat, tattoo, and taps. Despite the obvious benefit of practical skills, "in war, as in science, art, and literature, for the higher branches we must look to books—the recorded knowledge of the past." According to Sherman every officer, particularly those aspiring to high command and staff positions, needed broad military and educational experience. Literacy, some ability in mathematics, and a knowledge of geography and American history were prerequisites for every commissioned officer. Senior officers required familiarity with higher mathematics, chemistry, geology, and law.[5] Acknowledging the necessity of theoretical study, Sherman nonetheless emphasized the importance of practical work. He wanted school doctrine to rest on the premise that service with troops in peacetime was the most honorable duty an officer could perform, as well as the best preparation for high command in time of war.[6]

Although Sherman strongly believed in military education and did much to improve the quality of the officer corps, he admitted that something less than high ideals actually prompted the order that had established the school: "I confess I made the order as a concession to the everlasting demands of friends and families to have their boys detailed to Signal duty, or to the School at Fort Monroe to escape company duty in the Indian country. The School at Leavenworth may do some good, and be a safety-valve for those who are resolved to escape from the drudgery of garrison life at small posts."[7] Thus in the short run Sherman gave in to the sort of sentiment that he was trying to eliminate in the long run.

There were other contradictions in his action. Although he wanted the school to prepare officers for high command, the officers assigned there were junior lieutenants whose greatest need was to develop competence in tactics, not strategy. Sherman's stress on broad education detracted from the effort to correct obvious military shortcomings among many officers. These divergent strains, running through the rationale behind the course, emphasized that Sherman founded the school as "an experiment only."[8] Initially the School of Application lacked a clearly defined purpose. Once in operation, however, the War Department would enlarge it, change its curriculum, or completely reorganize it as necessity dictated.

Sherman disapproved of the regulations and course of study prepared by the staff of the school. The regulations subordinated the designated commandant, Colonel Elwell S. Otis, to the staff while the course of study followed in great detail the curriculum then in force at the Artillery School. "Onerous" was the term Sherman used to describe the proposed regulations. He wrote Otis: "I prefer to make another General Order, which will enable you to put in operation the School, and to maintain that simple direct command and control so essential to all military success."[9]

Aware that the previous recommendations had not considered the background of potential students, Sherman outlined a two tract program. Depending on their past education and experience, the students would be divided into two groups: the first class and the second (or remedial) class. The course for each was two years. Normally students would remain in the class to which they were originally assigned. If second-class students at the end of one year had improved sufficiently, they could advance to the first class for the next year. The curriculum for the first class emphasized practical instruction in military subjects, such as organization, tactics, and drill. The second class also studied these subjects but concentrated on theoretical instruction that they should have received before commissioning, including reading, writing, grammar, arithmetic, geography, history, algebra, geometry, and trigonometry. As Sherman recognized, these were subjects that "every young gentleman should be presumed to know."[10]

The most pressing problem, one not solved for several years, was how to classify the students. Lacking guidelines for the selection of students, regimental commanders varied considerably in the quality of their appointments to the school. Some sent the regimental "idiot" or their biggest troublemaker, just to rid themselves of a problem for two years. Others selected their best officers, whom they thought could benefit from the school. Four infantry regiments sent no one. Some of the stu-

dents, recently commissioned from civilian life, had satisfactory
civil education but little knowledge of military affairs, while
others had only modest educational backgrounds but considerable military service. A third group consisted of West Point
graduates, a few of whom had participated in campaigns against
the Indians. On February 10, 1882, the school staff met to
examine and classify this diverse group of officers and to plan
class schedules and instruction methods.[11]

Normally there would be two terms during the school year,
which commenced in October and ended late in May, but the
abbreviated first year's course began March 11 and ended June
13. Both the first and second classes met twice daily, Monday
through Friday, for recitation sections on assigned texts. During this first year instructors gave few lectures and held no
demonstrations. The shortage of textbooks was so acute that
General Sherman sent his personal copy of Soady's *Lessons of
War* for use at the school.[12] The library existed in name only.
Qualified instructors were hard to find. Two students doubled
as teachers, one in military law, the other in geography. Before
the term began, school officials had recognized their difficult
situation. Limited instruction time necessitated omitting some
important subjects that Sherman had wanted included. But
Colonel Otis believed the course was the best that could be expected "under the circumstances."[13]

Practical instruction in basic military subjects was haphazard.
Without an established course of study, the commandant issued
periodic orders organizing special classes. The length of the
classes and the nature of the instruction varied. For instance,
one order emphasized the importance of bayonet training for
infantry officers and ordered all infantry lieutenants at the
school to attend a class in bayonet exercise. During the daily
hour of company drill, one student drilled the companies while
all others attended the bayonet class, conducted by another
student. A similar expedient was employed to begin a class in
the making of topographical surveys, which required students
to attend one hour of drawing practice daily.[14]

Several features characterized the curriculum for at least the
next six years. The course for the second class tried to correct

educational deficiencies at the expense of time spent on purely
military subjects. Because many of those in the second class
were only marginal officers, the time spent on remedial work
was probably not worth the effort and resources expended.
Purely military, and particularly tactical, instruction, even for
the first class, was simple and basic. Theoretical instruction
consisted of recitations on books that already were, or were
soon to become, obsolete (for instance, Dennis Hart Mahan's
primer *Outposts*, which first had appeared before the Civil War).
Practical work seldom went beyond the level of company, troop,
or battery drill. Overall the curriculum at the school in the years
from 1881 through 1887 was geared to preparing young subalterns for the duties they would face as company grade officers
in an army fast becoming administrative minded as its principal
operational opponent, the American Indian, became less of a
threat.

In July 1882 the school at Fort Leavenworth ended its first
term on a high note: all students had successfully completed
their exams. In their annual reports, two of the school's enthu-
siasts, Colonel Otis and General Pope, praised the progress made
and waxed optimistic about the future. Pope declared: "The
officers in charge of the school, and those sent here for instruction have been industrious and zealous in a remarkable degree,
and the progress made in the prescribed course, both theoretical
and practical, has been much beyond what anyone concerned
had anticipated."[15] Both Pope and Otis recommended expand-
ing the school and urged strong War Department support to
this end. As was often the case in annual reports, these two
officers were a bit too enthusiastic and overly optimistic. Sherman, more realistically, cautioned against "pushing this school
into the clouds."[16] Although he wanted to improve and expand
the facilities, he realized the necessity of subordinating its interests to the rest of the army. Having taken the initial step
to found the school, he recognized how far short it fell of his
original intention.

For several years after its inauguration, the scope of the
school remained limited. The diversity of backgrounds of the
students particularly inhibited progress. One critic complained:

"The curriculum of the second class at the infantry and cavalry school is a mortifying comment on the personnel of two important branches of the military service. It is the fault of a grossly deficient system of officering the army that it should be necessary to teach arithmetic and 'correct reading aloud' to officers who are employed in a profession which is daily becoming more scientific, and which is supposed to require a fair degree of ability and studious preparation on the part of its followers."[17] Largely because of the remedial nature of the second-class curriculum, the school in its early years acquired the derisive nickname "kindergarten." Even Colonel Otis admitted that in 1882 the course was only "fair."[18]

A contemporary observer wrote that some students and a few instructors doubted the value of the instruction.[19] One of the first graduates, William C. Brown, recalled fellow students struggling at the blackboard, unable to add two fractions. Many of those most needing instruction disliked the school, while others regarded it as a joke. When General Sherman heard of these attitudes, he personally addressed the students and told them if they did not do their work, they would be replaced. Brown remembered: "That plain talk from a man of General Sherman's prestige had a salutary effect."[20] But the effect did not last.

The second group of graduates disappointed Colonel Thomas H. Ruger, Otis's successor as commandant. Ten of forty students in that class failed their final exams and did not receive diplomas. Ruger found this remarkable because of the moderate demands made upon the students. He attributed the failures to neglect.[21] By 1885, when Ruger was commandant, the staff had begun a conscious effort to improve the school and overcome its poor reputation. To this end they gradually reduced the size of the second or remedial class, which in 1888 the War Department eliminated. Undoubtedly this helped raise the self-esteem and the reputation of the school. Furthermore Ruger admitted that the staff refused to grant diplomas to the ten students as a warning and to improve the motivation of future classes. In the future lackadaisical students would not graduate.

Gradually Leavenworth commandants were able to improve

the quality of instruction. With the support of three successive commanding generals of the army, Sherman, Sheridan, and Schofield, the commandants of the 1880s were able to secure the full-time assignment of a few instructors based on their qualifications and special aptitudes. The remainder of the instructors were drawn from officers already with units at the post whose principal responsibility was to the administration of those units, not to the school. According to Colonel Ruger, several of these officers "by physical disability and want of proper knowledge" were incompetent to teach any course.[22] Most, however, were competent enough field soldiers and small-unit administrators but had neither the educational background, broad military experience, nor dynamic personalities to be innovative, dynamic teachers. Direct assignment of even a limited few indicated the War Department would assist in improving the school.

Colonel Alexander McD. McCook, a famed Civil War corps commander who replaced Ruger as commandant in May 1886, continued the drive for reform by requesting all instructors, staff, and field officers at Leavenworth to submit recommendations for improvements. The general thrust of the suggestions was to make the course more rigorous, raise admission standards, require a greater quality of work from the students, and increase the amount of tactical training. General Sheridan used these recommendations as the basis for the school's first code of regulations, which in 1888 reorganized the course.

The new regulations abolished all remedial work and created seven academic departments, each with its own staff and curriculum: cavalry, infantry, artillery, law, engineering, hygiene, and military art. With the reorganization came a determination to emphasize practical application in the study of tactics, using field exercises when possible and map and terrain exercises without troops when studying operations of larger units.[23]

The adoption of the new curriculum and regulations, combined with the efforts of McCook to ensure that the system worked, marked the end of the "kindergarten" era at Leavenworth. McCook, a disciplinarian, perhaps even a martinet, began a strict regimen at Leavenworth. During his incumbency as commandant, school was in session six days a week; Saturday classes lasted until 5:00 P.M., two hours past the end of normal working days. The schedule demanded, as did McCook, that instructors work as hard as the students.[24]

The course pursued by the class that entered in September 1887 and graduated in June 1889 was representative of the emphasis on small-unit tactics characteristic of the curriculum until the Spanish War. Instruction was progressive, basic subjects preceding the more advanced. Daily recitation was an integral part of the course, although small-scale field problems were included.

The initial two-months' instruction was elementary and practical. Students were assigned to cavalry or infantry units at the post for drill and ceremonies, including guard mountings, reviews, parades, inspections, school of the soldier, and school of the company. Elementary tactics, essentially the use of proper formations, followed. Instruction in minor tactics, which integrated the study of cavalry, infantry, and artillery in attack and defense, concluded the initial tactical work. Once a week during September and October, the entire garrison and school held joint field exercises, pitting one group of students and garrison troops against another. Students assumed staff and command positions in the participating units and after each problem submitted reconnaissance sketches of the terrain traversed and reports analyzing the exercise.[25]

Instruction moved indoors during the winter when mapping, law, and hippology filled the course. Tactics again became the focus as spring approached. The work was more advanced than in the fall; the lectures, recitations, and problems considered forces up to the size of regiments. Field problems required students to analyze and solve tactical situations, often involving reconnaissance, security, attacks, or defense. Other outdoor work included surveying and topography, which the class concluded by preparing a hasty sketch map of the entire Leavenworth reservation. The first year's work ended in June with written and oral examinations in tactics, surveying, and topography.[26]

Following thirty days' leave, the class began its second year

of instruction in July 1888 and continued until June 1889. The
first three months were filled with practical work in signaling,
reconnaissance, and field engineering. Tactics resumed on September 25 with a two-week march to Topeka, Kansas. During
the five-day bivouac there, the command drilled extensively
and held several reviews and brigade formations. Upon their
return to Leavenworth, they continued practical work with
field problems and instructional rides, involving the attack and
defense of prepared positions, advance and rearguard formations, screening and reconnoitering. Understrength infantry
companies in the garrison, sometimes turning out only fifteen
enlisted men, diminished the realism of the exercises and im-
paired practical work.[27]

As in the previous year, theoretical instruction dominated
the winter months. Lectures and recitations on military history,
fire tactics, veterinary science, building superintendence, military hygiene, and international law filled the months until
outdoor work could resume. Engineering dominated the final
months of the course. Work was elementary but physically
demanding as students constructed shelter pits, trenches,
bridges, grabions, and hasty fieldworks. Two combined surveys
of portions of the Leavenworth reservation, using techniques
learned in the previous two years, concluded the practical work
in engineering. Final oral and written examinations again were
held during June.[28]

By the end of the 1880s, Leavenworth offered a thorough
and practical, though elementary, preparation in military tactics
and administration for junior officers. Graduates were qualified
"to survey and map any region; to make a reconnaissance either
mounted or on foot, and render a good field map and report of
the result; to construct field fortifications and military bridges;
to drill a company, troop or battalion; to command an outpost,
an advanced guard, or a rear guard; to adopt the tactics of his
own arm to the terrain on which he may be using it; and much
else that may be of inestimable value to him in the present
duties of war."[29] Instruction methods and course content were
concrete and involved little theorizing or abstraction. The emphasis was on problems with which troop leaders had to contend

within their own sight and hearing—within the limits they could personally control.

Every two years the Infantry and Cavalry School graduated about thirty lieutenants who had the potential to become good company-grade officers. For the moment the instruction adequately satisfied the needs of the army. The legacy of small-unit action and company size garrisons, characteristic of the Indian fighting army, had yet to give way to Mahanite preparations for overseas expeditionary forces. There was no demand to train officers in general staff duties because there was as yet no army General Staff. Because the army was small—it had only ten cavalry and twenty-five infantry regiments—there were few opportunities to command large units. A regiment was the largest unit an officer could reasonably expect to command during his career because of slow promotions, retirements only in old age, and the resulting stagnation within the officer corps. Postgraduate education of line officers, therefore, could logically stress preparation in small-unit tactics and company administration and well meet the needs of individual officers and the army. Not everyone was content with such an approach, however, which served only to maintain the status quo. In the decade before the Spanish War several instructors at Leavenworth tried to broaden the outlook of the students and prepare them for positions in a larger army with an expanded role.

NOTES

1. Emory Upton, *The Armies of Asia and Europe* (New York: D. Appleton and Co., 1878), p. 366.
2. Report of the Commander of the Department of the Missouri, *Annual Reports of the War Department* (Washington, D.C.: GPO, 1877), 1: 62, 64. Also see Charles King, "The Leavenworth School," *Harpers* 76 (April 1888): 778; and, "The General Service and Staff College: Historical Sketch," *Cavalry Journal* 13 (April 1903): 56. During these years elements of a single regiment were often stationed at widely separated posts. To concentrate two or three regiments at one post was a novel experiment indeed.
3. Samuel P. Huntington, *The Soldier and the State* (Cambridge, Mass.: Harvard University Press, 1957), p. 240.

4. General Orders No. 4, War Department, May 7, 1881; Report of the Commanding General, *Annual Reports of the War Department* (Washington, D.C.: GPO, 1882), 1: 39.

5. William T. Sherman, *Address to the School of Application* (Fort Leavenworth: School of Application, 1882), pp. 1-13.

6. Sherman to Sheridan, November 22, 1881, letterbook 95, William T. Sherman Papers, Library of Congress.

7. Ibid., July 31, 1881, letterbook 95, Sherman Papers.

8. Eben Swift, "An American Pioneer in the Cause of Military Education," *Journal of the Military Service Institution* 44 (January-February 1909): 69.

9. Sherman to Otis, January 26, 1882, letterbook 95, Sherman Papers.

10. General Orders No. 8, War Department, January 26, 1882.

11. Report of the Commandant, *Annual Reports of the War Department* (Washington, D.C.: GPO, 1882), 1: 176. The first class (1882-83) included thirty-five officers, twenty in the first class and fifteen in the second class. There were seven West Pointers, five commissioned from the ranks, and twenty-three commissioned from civilian life. Length of service ranged from one who had served fifteen years to five who had served less than a year.

12. William C. Brown, "General Sherman and the Infantry and Cavalry School," *Cavalry Journal* 16 (July 1905): 124.

13. *Annual Reports* (1882), pp. 176-77.

14. Orders No. 188, Fort Leavenworth, August 11, 1882; Orders No. 205, Fort Leavenworth, September 4, 1882, Adjutant General's Office Letters Received, Record Group 94, National Archives.

15. *Annual Reports* (1882), p. 102.

16. Adjutant General to General Pope, October 4, 1882, file 4062, RG 94.

17. Arthur L. Wagner, "The Military Necessities of the United States," *Journal of the Military Service Institution* 5 (September 1884): 262.

18. Inspection report by Colonel Otis, September 24, 1882, file 1062/82, Letters Received by the Inspector General's Office, RG 159, National Archives.

19. King, "Leavenworth School," pp. 779-80.

20. William C. Brown quoted in George F. Brimlow, *Cavalryman out of the West: The Life of General William Cary Brown* (Caldwell, Idaho: Caxton Printers, 1944), pp. 107-8.

21. Report of the Commandant, *Annual Reports of the War Department* (Washington, D.C.: GPO, 1885), 1: 211-14.

22. Ibid. (1886), 1: 211.

23. Elvid Hunt, *The History of Fort Leavenworth* (Fort Leavenworth: Army Service Schools Press, 1926), pp. 168-70; *Annual Reports* (1886), pp. 211-12; Report of General Sheridan, November 1, 1887, file 5445, RG 94.

24. Report of the Commandant, *Annual Reports of the War Department* (Washington, D.C.: GPO, 1888), 1: 194; Historical Sketch 1895, file 25472, RG 94; E. R. Hagemann, ed., *Fighting Rebels and Redskins: Experiences in the Army Life of Colonel George B. Sanford* (Norman: University of Oklahoma Press, 1969), pp. 72-73.

25. *Annual Reports* (1888), pp. 194-95. Among the problems were calculating time and space occupied in the movement of troops, advanced guard opposing an advanced guard, posting of outposts, infantry patrol against an advanced guard, meeting engagement of two infantry patrols, cavalry squadron against a cavalry troop, and two forces of combined arms and rear guard against an advanced guard.

26. Ibid., p. 195.

27. Report of the Commandant, *Annual Reports of the War Department* (Washington, D.C.: GPO, 1889), 1: 202; Major Hamilton S. Hawkins to Post Adjutant, December 18, 1887, file 98, RG 94.

28. *Annual Reports* (1889), 1: 202-05.

29. Arthur L. Wagner, "An American War College," *Journal of the Military Service Institution* 10 (July 1889): 290.

3

THE ERA OF
WAGNER AND SWIFT

During the tenure of John M. Schofield as commanding general (1888-95), the army undertook several reforms that improved the tactical organization of the service and raised the quality of the officer corps. Most of the ideas implemented had been encouraged for years by the Uptonian reformers. The evolution to a more militarily active, expansionist, Mahanite national strategy required an army that was more than a frontier constabulary. Schofield was committed to the reforms. Thus by the 1890s the climate had improved for their acceptance.[1]

Among the changes made were examination on professional subjects before promotion up to and including the rank of major, promotion within the branch of service rather than within the regiment, and compilation of annual officer efficiency reports. The examinations and efficiency reports put officers on notice that their ability and performance were a matter of concern; to remain public servants, they had to meet certain minimum standards. The improved promotion system was an incentive needed to keep promising officers in the army.

While Schofield was commanding general, the War Department opened a school of application for cavalry and light artillery at Fort Riley, began a lyceum system within each regiment in which junior officers were to receive basic military instruction, and continued to urge support from the army and Congress for the schools at Leavenworth and Fort Monroe. Although Congress had authorized the Riley institution in 1887 and the impact of the lyceums was dubious, Schofield impressed young officers with the benefits of advanced training and created an atmosphere within the army sympathetic to the needs of military education.[2] Leavenworth prospered in such an atmosphere. Several vigorous commandants and a number of outstanding instructors improved the quality of the curriculum and the image of the school.

During his last year as commandant, Colonel McCook reduced the time devoted to elementary tactics by requiring potential students to pass an examination in drill regulations and tactics up to battalion level before entering the school. Instruction in advanced tactics and military history filled the time thus saved. Colonel Edwin F. Townsend, who succeeded McCook in August 1890, initiated other changes. For instance, without changing the curriculum he eliminated several of the academic departments and streamlined administration. The commandant from 1894 to 1898, Colonel Hamilton S. Hawkins, continued improvements in a manner similar to those of his predecessors. He eliminated all remedial work; students not able to meet the rigors of the course were not admitted. More significantly Hawkins improved instruction methods by abolishing daily recitations and encouraging a freer exchange between students and faculty. Recitations, he believed, were a remnant of the early years of the school when "no one knew what else to turn his hand to in making a beginning."[3]

By the mid-1890s Leavenworth had changed considerably from the early years when the tendency was to reach for something tangible, as manifested in the emphasis on drill, ceremonies, and garrison duties. In the early years the focus of instruction was narrow, a legacy of the army's garrison mentality. Leavenworth had considered itself the ideal post to train subalterns in all the duties they could expect to face in their early careers. Such a concept, however, tended to limit the thinking and vision of students and instructors to the dimensions of the fort.

While McCook, Townsend, and Hawkins tried to broaden the

impact of the school, substantive change came as a result of
improvements in the curriculum and instruction. Two instructors, Arthur L. Wagner and Eben Swift, made the greatest contribution to the evolution of Leavenworth during the late 1880s
and the 1890s. Their work laid the basis for Leavenworth methods, course content, doctrine, and overall objectives until World
War I. Wagner and Swift were the catalysts in breaking down the
garrison mentality at the school. Their concerns were more ab-
stract, more theoretical—a sign of the course's growing sophistica-
tion. They attempted to look beyond the mere functioning of
lieutenants as tacticians and administrators in infantry companies or cavalry troops. During the era when Wagner and Swift
taught, Leavenworth became a fount for new and original military thinking in the army. The school became more than a
model post and contributed more to the service than simply
thirty competent lieutenants graduated every two years.

Arthur L. Wagner joined the Leavenworth faculty in 1886
and served, with several interruptions, until 1903 as assistant
instructor, senior instructor, and assistant commandant. Certain
features colored his military career and distinguished him as
one of the reform-minded group taking its lead from Sherman
and Upton. As a student at West Point his interests had ranged
beyond the formal aspects of the curriculum; he studied military history and worked on cadet literary publications. These
outside interests hurt his final standing in the class of 1875,
which was forty out of forty-three, but later served him well.
Commissioned in the Sixth Infantry, he spent the next six
years with his regiment on the frontier. Between 1881 and
1885 he was professor of military science and tactics at Louisiana State University and at East Florida Seminary. During this
period he wrote an essay, "The Military Necessities of the
United States and the Best Method of Meeting Them," which
won a gold medal from the Military Service Institution of the
United States. A fellow officer wrote that Wagner's essay "was
a powerful statement, was widely read and certainly exercised
some influence."[4] Wagner rejoined his regiment in 1885 at
Fort Douglas, Utah. One year later the War Department rede-
ployed the Sixth Infantry to Fort Leavenworth. The comman-

dant of the school, then Colonel McCook, requested Wagner
as an assistant instructor because of his interest in history, literary success, prior teaching experience, and "special liking"
for the study of the art of war.[5]

A trip to Europe to study Prussian military schools, the German Army, and various military campaigns furnished material
for Wagner's first book, *The Campaign of Königgrätz*, published
in 1889. While teaching at Leavenworth, he wrote two other
books, which remained standard military works for many years,
The Service of Security and Information (1893) and *Organization and Tactics* (1895). In 1894 Wagner, then a captain, succeeded Lieutenant Colonel Jacob Kline as head of the department of military art. Colonel Townsend commended Wagner
for the "untiring zeal" he brought to the department.[6]

Leaving the school in 1896 Wagner became chief of the Military Information Division of the Adjutant General's Office and
in that position helped to gather intelligence and formulate
plans for the campaign against Cuba in 1898. During the Santiago campaign he distinguished himself by making two important reconnaissances under enemy fire. He later served as a staff
officer in Puerto Rico and the Philippines and returned to Leavenworth in 1903 as assistant commandant. When he died in
1905, Wagner was senior director of the newly established Army
War College and chief of the Third Division of the War Department General Staff. For half of his thirty-year career, Wagner
was involved in military education, ten years at Leavenworth.

According to an officer who met him in the early 1900s,
Wagner was "a friendly old man who looked like a farmer
dressed up in a uniform."[7] His easy, friendly manner was an
asset in imparting his own tactical and technical knowledge to
the students. It was also somewhat misleading, for Wagner was
a serious-minded student of the military profession. That he
published a number of articles and books in a relatively short
time indicates the effort he put into his work. But there was
another side to him. He craved recognition for his many accomplishments and worked particularly hard for that most obvious symbol of recognition in the military: promotion. On a
number of occasions when he sought vacancies in staff depart-

ments, which if granted would have meant a promotion, Wagner
solicited endorsements from friends, former commanders, poli-
ticians, and even his father-in-law.[8] Other officers tried to mus-
ter influence and support when seeking promotions and assignments, but Wagner's efforts appear more systematic and wide
ranging, including printed excerpts from the most laudatory
letters and efficiency reports.

Wagner's quest for recognition and promotion stemmed from
an insecurity bred of ridicule and criticism. One young officer
remembered that many senior officers opposed any studious preparation and "damned him as being an impractical sort of officer."[9] The charge of being a "mere theorist" rankled Wagner,
who attributed the opposition to his promotion on several occasions to this inaccurate accusation.[10]

As a young lieutenant he had taken part in the Sioux and Nez
Perce campaigns of the late 1870s. He later helped construct
telegraph lines in Dakota and Colorado and again in 1881 served
on active operations against the Utes. As a staff officer in Cuba
and the Philippines, he had also smelled gunpowder. Similarly
his writings were based largely on his own experience and historical precedents, not theorizing. Wagner was no Clausewitz,
not even a Mahan. His works were intended as practical guides
for field operations. Because he was truly a pioneer and so pro-
digious an author, he became a natural target for the anti-intellectual officers who distrusted any sort of "book learning."

Despite the debunkers, Wagner's teaching, writing, and military ability generally were appreciated. Two Leavenworth commandants, McCook and Hawkins, thought he was an excellent
officer. Each had commanded him on troop duty as well as at
the school and found him to be as good a leader and field soldier
as teacher. Hawkins characterized him as "an officer of great
ability."[11] Because of his knowledge of general staff procedures,
based on observation and study of the German system and experience in the Military Information Division, the War Department selected Wagner for an important position on the General
Staff shortly after it was organized. Similarly his depth of knowledge and broad experience as a tactician were the reasons the
department appointed him chief umpire at the joint army-

militia maneuvers in 1902, 1903, and 1904. He was superb at analyzing a unit's performance in the field and at suggesting means for improving performance. The reports he prepared on the Santiago campaign and the joint maneuvers testified to this ability and were significant documents as critiques of the state of the military art in the United States Army at the turn of the century.

Contemporaries and historians alike have acknowledged Wagner's contribution to the army. General J. Franklin Bell spoke for many army progressives when he declared that more than any other officer of his era Wagner encouraged "acquirement of military knowledge."[12] An early historian of the American army, William A. Ganoe, also praised Wagner with awakening officers to the need for "endless study and practice," which contributed immeasurably to battlefield success in World War I.[13] More recently Russell F. Weigley credited him with cultivating "high standards of military scholarship and stimulating teaching" at Leavenworth.[14] From about 1890 until his death Wagner's name was synonymous with tactical instruction and the Leavenworth schools.

While at Leavenworth Wagner attempted to make the study of tactics more interesting. One Leavenworth graduate believed Wagner was "the first of our military men to write anything readable on tactics."[15] Because he thought the purpose of the school was to improve an officer's efficiency as a leader, not merely to fill his head with facts, Wagner emphasized an analytical approach in studying tactics. Under his direction the department of military art began using the applicatory method of instruction, an instructional technique developed in the German Army, refined and adapted to American needs by Wagner's assistant, Eben Swift. Increasingly the department used map problems, map maneuvers (also called war games), and tactical rides (terrain exercises) and stressed the systematic issuance of orders.

Wagner's influence on Leavenworth students was great, and through his writings he influenced the rest of the army as well. By explaining recent European military experiences and relating them to American experience and doctrine, Wagner's writing

was an important part of the growing professionalization of the
United States Army. The number of foreign sources cited in
his works testify to his wide reading and breadth of knowledge.
The German theorists—von Schellendorff on staff duties, von
Scherff on infantry tactics, von Schell on artillery—were difficult for many officers to comprehend, even in translation.
Wagner studied the Europeans, synthesized their work, and
wrote his own books with American organization, tactics, and
experiences in mind. His friend and fellow instructor, Eben
Swift, reported: "The army became students at once, and Wagner's books became as familiar as the drill books."[16] Wagner
was more than a mere paraphraser of Europeans, for many
he was the final American arbiter on military tactics and strategy. What Upton had done in the sphere of military organization and policy, Wagner did for tactics.

Wagner's three principal works, *The Campaign of Königgrätz*,
Security and Information, and *Organization and Tactics*, were
a direct result of his instruction at Leavenworth. When he found
no satisfactory textbooks on tactics, strategy, military organization, and military history, he wrote his own. All three books
included variations on several themes that were the heart of
Wagner's military thought.

Wagner believed that, with the exception of actual experience
in war, a critical analysis of recent military history offered the
best prospect for acquiring knowledge of organization and tactics. The success of the Prussian Army in 1866 and 1870 greatly
impressed him, especially the decisive battle at Königgrätz. His
book on the campaign was a detailed study that analyzed the
strengths and weaknesses of the opposing armies. Wagner pointed
out object lessons for American officers—for instance, the contrasting command arrangements of the opposing forces. On the
Austrian side responsibility for decision making rested solely
with the Austrian commander, von Benedek. The Prussians, on
the other hand, delegated considerable responsibility, from the
emperor to the lowest foot soldier. In the crisis of battle the
Prussians were better able to adjust to the changing situation,
while the subordinate Austrian commanders, not even fully
aware of von Benedek's plans, were unable to react.[17]

Organization and strategy were of interest to Wagner, but tactics was his real concern. He observed that the Prussians in 1866 had attacked in formation of company, half-battalion, or battalion columns, preceded by weak lines of skirmishers. Although columns enabled the Prussians to gain rapid numerical superiority at key points, the enemy could concentrate fire, causing many casualties. Columns were also difficult formations from which to establish fire superiority. Despite heavy casualties the Prussians retained the column as their principal attack formation until 1870 when the Prussian Guards were decimated at St. Privat. These tactics did not impress Wagner who considered the formations used in the American Civil War superior and not that much changed over thirty years. By the end of the war, Union divisions had attacked in three lines of brigades, about 150 yards separating each line, with the leading brigade preceded by several lines of skirmishers. As the assault progressed, the first brigade absorbed the lines of skirmishers, and the succeeding lines of brigades reinforced the first line. The Americans did not advance totally in the open but took advantage of the shape of the ground and the cover it offered. In 1889, when Wagner wrote *Königgrätz*, Germany Army doctrine required attack formations similar to what the Americans had adopted by 1864.

Wagner concluded that recent American experience offered as many lessons for the Europeans as their wars did for United States Army officers. The Austrians, for instance, were totally ignorant of hasty entrenchments, which were used extensively by both sides in the Civil War. Had the Austrians entrenched in 1866, they might have more effectively resisted the Prussians. But Wagner was not parochial; his intent was not to make a case for American tactical superiority. As a means of instruction he would describe both American and European methods and analyze their strengths and weaknesses.[18]

Wagner's second book, *The Service of Security and Information* (1893), continued in this vein. The author endeavored "to select the best established theories of European tactical authorities, to illustrate them by reference to events in our own military history, and to apply to them the touchstone of American practice in war."[19] As described by Wagner, security and information were the basic tactical functions. They were inseparable because to protect friendly forces it was necessary to be informed of energy dispositions and intentions. To gain information by reconnaissances, friendly troops quickly had to establish and maintain contact with the enemy. Cavalry formations preceded the main force, made contact with the advance parties of the enemy, and tried to brush aside or push them back into the main enemy formation. The cavalry in this way prevented the enemy from penetrating to the principal friendly force. Infantry and artillery also could be used in the more static role of outposts, pickets, and screens.[20]

In *Security and Information* Wagner described the proper organization and functions of these reconnaissance forces when in contact with the enemy. He included a wealth of useful information, from practical tips on the amount of noise and dust created by a marching column, to an analysis of the information that could be derived from inhabitants of enemy territory, to the proper tactics used when encountering an enemy patrol. Wagner used history throughout, sometimes to illustrate self-evident conclusions and sometimes to analyze a not-so-obvious conclusion. He was not at all dogmatic and emphasized that flexibility was the greatest lesson to be learned. In the 1903 revised edition, for example, he noted how the jungle terrain recently encountered in Cuba and the Philippines had necessitated alterations in standard tactical formations.[21] Security and information were only a small part of what officers needed to know to be competent tacticians. They were useful subjects for dealing with initial encounters with the enemy, but they were only the first steps.

Wagner's third major work, *Organization and Tactics* (1895), dealt at length with the tactical employment of infantry, cavalry, and artillery in attack and defense. Again Wagner relied heavily on military history to provide lessons; over a quarter of the book described the evolution of infantry, cavalry, and artillery tactics during the previous century. Once more he reiterated the theme that American officers should study European developments in light of the Civil War because "scarcely a feature of the tactics of the present day . . . did not have its germ, its prototype, or development in that great contest."[22] According to Wagner the principal tactical developments of that conflict were attacks by rushes, attacks in successive deployed lines, use of heavy lines of skirmishers, and use of hasty entrenchments. His history, however, was secondary to his discussion of tactical employment on the battlefield.

Although Wagner believed that only offensive action resulted in a decisive result, he admitted that improved range and accuracy of infantry and artillery weapons had strengthened the defensive "enormously."[23] Frontal assaults, although possible, were becoming more costly, especially against an entrenched enemy. Unless the assailant had great morale and numerical superiority, a frontal assault would fail. To succeed attacks had to be well supported, well led, and adapted to the conditions at hand to take advantage of enemy weak points and cover. He thought attacks should attempt to envelop a flank or attack from the rear whenever possible. An attacking unit would advance by successive movements from a point perhaps 3,000 yards from the enemy position in extended, open formation to the final assault in which the troops would most likely form a single, dense line. He believed that successful tactics required taking advantage of any weakness the enemy showed. He stressed flexibility, not rigid doctrine.[24]

Not surprisingly the emphasis on flexibility was a result of the eclectic nature of Wagner's study. In his analysis of recent European and American experience, he could often draw no hard conclusions. He was conscious that military history could be interpreted to demonstrate almost any point; consequently it had to be used cautiously. He wanted to immerse officers in the details of a variety of tactical situations, where they could draw their own conclusions regarding a proper course to be pursued. Because history offered an infinite variety of tactical situations to be analyzed, it became Wagner's principal means of instruction.

Captain Eben Swift, who had a somewhat different career from his colleague, also played an important role in the transformation of Leavenworth. Graduating from West Point in time for the Big Horn and Yellowstone campaigns in 1876, Swift

spent seventeen years with his regiment in the West. His only
detour from line duty was as aide-de-camp to General Wesley
Merritt. In 1893 Swift went to Leavenworth and remained there
until 1897 as one of Wagner's assistant instructors. Two other
times in his career Swift returned to the school: from 1904 to
1906 as senior instructor in military art and as assistant commandant and for a short time in 1916 as commandant.

During the Spanish War and immediately thereafter, Swift
served with Volunteer units. Before returning to Leavenworth
in 1904 he spent a year as an assistant adjutant general. After
leaving the school in 1906 he went to the Army War College
as director. His subsequent service was commanding a regiment
in the Philippines and two years as chief of staff of the Western
Department. Swift managed to get into the last months of the
Mexican Punitive Expedition as commander of a provisional
cavalry division. During World War I he held several positions,
including commanding general of a training division, observer
with the French Army, and head of the American military mission to Italy. He retired in 1918.[25]

In several ways Swift was an interesting contrast to Wagner.
Whereas Wagner's tastes and diversions were literary, Swift enjoyed riding and shooting. Little beyond professional military
subjects interested him (Wagner had commercial interests).
Officers who knew both used terms such as "brilliant" and "all-
around ability" to describe Wagner; "a good soldier" and
"studious" were more descriptive of Swift. On Swift's 1895
efficiency report Hawkins wrote: "Is reliable; good judgment;
good ability; not quick, but gets there." There was no question
about his knowledge or ability. But to reach the same level,
Swift probably had to work harder and apply himself more
diligently than Wagner.[26]

Like Wagner, Swift had a reputation as a "book soldier."
As if to confirm that reputation, he proclaimed in an unpublished memoir that he knew more about military history, particularly the Civil War, than any other officer in the army.
Because of his great wealth of knowledge Swift believed the
War Department should have given him a combat command
during World War I.[27]

Perhaps the inappropriate connection between knowledge and command were the result of nostalgic musings by a retired, passed-over general. It is doubtful, however, that Wagner would have conceived such a conundrum, for he recognized the distinction between competent commanders and military intellectuals. Wagner bridged this gap; Swift was not as successful in doing so. When the War Department planned to make Swift commander of a cavalry regiment in 1914, a young Leavenworth-trained officer in that regiment vigorously protested to a friend on the General Staff: "As you know colonel [*sic*] Swift is a saturated solution of Civil War History and while that is a fine thing in its place I am sure we need a very different kind of colonel here. Please give us a live one."[28] Notwithstanding these shortcomings, Swift was a good officer, made significant contributions to tactical instruction throughout the army, and was instrumental in creating a distinctive Leavenworth doctrine.

Swift introduced the applicatory method of tactical instruction to Leavenworth. In July 1893 Wagner and Swift both agreed that the course required more practical work, particularly additional tactical problem solving. Wagner, as senior military art instructor, charged Swift with preparing all practical work in the department, which he did between 1893 and 1897. Later, from 1907 to 1910, he established a smiliar system of instruction at the Army War College. Wagner gave considerable credit to Swift and in 1894 attributed the success of the entire department to Swift's "able and zealous efforts."[29] Prior to Swift's arrival most practical instruction had been "sham battles" between groups of students, or very simple map exercises, which usually required explanations of the situation, not clear solutions framed in the form of written orders.

Swift acknowledged that the intellectual basis of the applicatory method he introduced was not the result of original thinking: "It was well known and practiced for more than 30 years when we took it up."[30] The basic elements of the applicatory method went back to the days of Frederick the Great and in recent years had been refined in the German Army by Von Verdy du Vernois and Otto F. Griepenkerl. Because he did not know German, Swift used French translations of their work.

Swift traced numerous battlefield failures to a misunderstanding of orders, which he attributed to the absence of a systematic means of issuing orders. Historically commanders either had prescribed in great detail the execution of an order or had merely pointed out the objective, leaving the execution entirely to the judgment of subordinates. Neither extreme satisfied Swift. Based on German techniques for troop leading, he developed a system of tactical orders, or "simple tactical forms," to meet every situation. Each form, a five-paragraph order, would contain the following information: the general situation, including information on enemy and friendly forces; the objective; disposition of troops and tasks assigned to each of the several factions of the command; instructions for logistic support of the operation; and instruction for communications during the operation.[31] The form provided a shortcut to problem solving by including all pertinent information without deluging commanders with extraneous details. Within clearly delineated limits, the guidelines allowed subordinates to carry out the plan by their own means, thus relieving the overall commander from a mass of routine work. By standardizing tactical practices, the field order contributed to a better understanding among officers. It encouraged uniform doctrine and established standard tactical terminology, an obvious advantage in the stress and confusion of war.

Swift's system became an essential part of the applicatory method used at Leavenworth. Each of the five paragraphs of the field order considered one important aspect of any tactical situation. Officers dealing with the simplest or most complex situation, in a map exercise or a field problem, had to consider these five aspects. The system provided a shortcut and a standard for training as it did for decision making in the field. Before writing an order, each student studied the map, made an estimate of the situation, and then made a tactical decision, using the five parts of the order as a guide. Instruction became more a test of decision making and judgment than of academic attainment.

While at Leavenworth Swift took the lead among American officers in refining and adopting the German *kriegsspiel* for use

by the U.S. Army. War gaming had evolved over the course of
a century from an exercise resembling chess to a complex pro-
cedure. By the late nineteenth century two basic forms existed.
"Rigid *kriegsspiel*" entailed many rules and accurate tables of
statistics, culled from experience in the Franco-Prussian War,
which governed moves on the map and the outcome of the
game (the tables included such data as how fast a particular
sized unit could move a certain distance under various weather
conditions or the killing power of a particular weapon at a
specified distance from the target). "Free *kriegsspiel*" abandoned the numerous rules and tables and relied instead on rules
extemporized by the director of the game on the spot. The
free version emphasized the soundness of a particular decision
in contrast to rigid *kriegsspiel*, which required complicated
calculations to determine the exact number of enemy put out
of action. Swift was the leading American proponent of free
kriegsspiel. Under his prodding, the Infantry and Cavalry School
adopted the system outlined by Von Verdy du Vernois in *A Simplified War Game*. Of the new methods Swift wrote: "After
hard struggles with many systems, my experience led me to believe that this was the only system that could be successfully
applied by American students, and I trust that it will find its
welcome in the reaction against text-book instruction and essay
writing in our service."[32]

The introduction of the applicatory method, the use of *kriegsspiel*, and the adoption of the standard form for field orders began on February 7, 1894, when Swift lectured on map maneuvers. Several simple map exercises followed. Another lecture
(on April 2), which established the standard form for field
orders and messages, was his most significant because it laid the
basis for all that followed. Tactical rides, which were problem-
solving exercises in the field without troops, were held in April
and June. A map exercise in June 1894 was the "first problem
of the kind, requiring the systematic issue of orders." The problem, solved on a map of Leavenworth, involved the march of
an infantry brigade from the fort against an enemy force on
Big Stranger Creek. From this modest beginning of two lectures
and a dozen problems, under Swift's guidance the system grew.

Two years later the course included six lectures and eighty exercises.[33]

When the War Department wanted to relieve both Swift and Wagner early in 1897, Colonel Hawkins strongly protested. He credited both with great contributions to the school and particularly praised Swift's work with the practical problems, work for which he had previously received little recognition.[34]

Wagner and Swift were more important for their ideas and approach to military education than for the specific information they may have passed on to their students. Their work at Leavenworth came at a most propitious time—the school and the army were ready for change. In their attempt to get students to think about their profession and in introducing the applicatory method, Wagner and Swift moved Leavenworth beyond a mere school of application that trained officers for their next assignment. The skills they taught would be useful throughout a military career. By 1898 a distinctive Leavenworth doctrine was emerging. The rest of the army was beginning to take notice of the school, its graduates, and of the writings of its two most prominent faculty: Wagner and Swift.

During its first years many considered remedying the educational defects of officers, some with only an elementary school education, the primary objective of Leavenworth. Because of its reputation as a kindergarten, officers often resented assignment to the school. In time, with the elimination of remedial subjects and upgrading of curriculum and instructional methods, the reputation improved. Officers actively sought to become students. General Schofield noted the steady development: "Its opportunities are now sought for by young officers, as a means of gaining that higher education which is essential to the satisfactory performance of the higher duties of the staff, and of the command of large bodies of troops in time of war."[35] Captain William H. Carter agreed. He reported in 1894 that a majority of young officers were anxious to attend the school and to test their skill against their peers.[36] Another young officer, Lieutenant Elmer Hubbard, thought that most officers regarded advanced training of the sort offered at Leavenworth an essential part of their careers.[37]

War Department officials also reflected the changing attitude toward the school and recognized its usefulness to the service, as well as its benefit to individual officers. One senior general reported in 1896: "The alumni of the school are held in special esteem; the honor of a diploma from the Artillery School and the Infantry and Cavalry School as a testimonial of ability and acquirements, is appreciated by the officers of the service and by civilians."[38] His assessment was no doubt true in a general way. But when it came to making use of Leavenworth-trained officers in time of emergency, the story was different. Serving in the adjutant general's office at the time of the outbreak of war with Spain, Captain Carter had access to the personnel records of all Leavenworth graduates, which included recommendations by the school staff on how each graduate could best be employed in time of war. Despite Carter's urging, the War Department made assignments without reference to these recommendations.[39] In 1898 most of the army was not antagonistic to the school, merely apathetic; it had yet to adjust its bureaucracy to take advantage of Leavenworth-trained officers.

Problems at the school itself also limited its effect on the Army. The greatest difficulty for many years was the uncertainty among school officials as to their task. Too often they attempted more than they were capable of doing. Originally this was manifest in the first-class—second-class dichotomy. Vestiges of this problem remained until the end of the century. While Wagner and his colleagues tried to make it a war college, some critics insisted this was not the proper course. Captain James S. Pettit suggested that Leavenworth tried to accomplish two goals but succeeded in neither: "If it is to remain a school for young lieutenants of various and unknown abilities, it should retain its name and make the course adhere to the needs and abilities of the students. If it is to be made a 'War College'. . . . then it should have selected students, officers of rank and experience, who can demonstrate that they can give two years' time to the study and investigation of the highest and most intricate features of military art and science. It seems to me that middle ground would be temporizing with military education."[40] Pettit saw the crux of the problem: it was difficult to study both with satisfactory results.

The army needed an entire system of postgraduate schools to instruct in all aspects of military art, tactics as well as strategy. Sherman had realized the School of Application could not provide fundamental instruction for junior lieutenants and conduct worthwhile courses in grand tactics, logistics, and strategy. Although Secretary of War Elihu Root established a comprehensive educational system after the Spanish-American War that eventually solved this problem, between 1881 and 1898 the unclear purpose of the school was apparent on several levels. Officers selected to attend Leavenworth in order to obtain a basic knowledge of military affairs were unprepared for more advanced study. Most important was the influence of the graduates on the army. Even if the students could understand the subject matter, what practical use was instruction in strategy or logistics to a junior second lieutenant? Graduates of the school had little opportunity to apply such learning.

Over the course of seventeen years, the school at Fort Leavenworth had greatly improved its curriculum, instructional methods, and the quality of students and instructors. But the ambivalent nature of the institution, neither training school nor war college, tended to reduce its overall impact on the army.

NOTES

1. The most sophisticated, detailed treatment of army reform during these years is Graham A. Cosmas, *An Army for Empire: The United States Army in the Spanish-American War* (Columbia: University of Missouri Press, 1971), chaps. 1-3. This account is particularly worthwhile for placing army reform within the context of the changing national strategy. Other accounts include William A. Ganoe, *The History of the United States Army*, rev. ed. (Ashton, Md.: Eric Lundberg, 1964), pp. 363-70; Russell F. Weigley, "The Military Thought of John M. Schofield," *Military Affairs* 23 (Summer 1958-59): 77-84; and Russell F. Weigley, *History of the United States Army* (New York: Macmillan, 1967), chap. 12.

2. The Fourteenth Infantry school at Vancouver Barracks in 1898 was held once a week at the officers' club. Instruction consisted of officers'

reading research papers on a topic of their own choosing. An officer who was there remembered some of the papers were well received, but he doubted that the lyceum had improved his ability to command a small unit in combat. Perry L. Miles, *Fallen Leaves: Memories of an Old Soldier* (Berkeley, Calif.: Wuerth Publishing Co., 1961), p. 3.

3. See reports of the respective commandants in *Annual Reports of the War Department* (Washington, D.C.: GPO, 1889), 1: 205; ibid. (1891), 1: 264; ibid. (1892), p. 143; ibid. (1895), 1: 177-78.

4. Eben Swift, "An American Pioneer in the Cause of Military Education," *Journal of the Military Service Institution* 44 (January-February 1909): 67.

5. McCook to Adjutant General, October 3, 1886, file 2908-ACP-1882, Record Group 94, National Archives.

6. Report of the Commandant, *Annual Reports of the War Department* (Washington, D.C.: GPO, 1894), 1: 169.

7. Charles D. Herron quoted in Forrest C. Pogue, *George C. Marshall: Education of a General* (New York: Viking Press, 1963), p. 94.

8. See file 2908-ACP-1882, RG 94.

9. George C. Marshall interview with Forrest Pogue, April 4, 1957. I have notes of transcripts of this and subsequently cited interviews by Dr. Pogue.

10. Wagner to J. Franklin Bell, April 28, 1904, file 2908-ACP-1882, RG 94.

11. Hawkins, Efficiency Report on Wagner, June 30, 1897; also McCook to Adjutant General, October 4, 1896; Hawkins to Adjutant General, November 25, 1902, file 2908-ACP-1882, RG 94.

12. Bell to Adjutant General, June 18, 1903, file 2908-ACP-1882, RG 94.

13. Ganoe, *History*, p. 423.

14. Weigley, *History*, p. 326.

15. Herron, quoted in Pogue, *Education of a General*, p. 94.

16. Swift, "American Pioneer," p. 71.

17. Arthur L. Wagner, *The Campaign of Königgrätz* (Leavenworth: C. J. Smith and Co., 1889), p. 73.

18. Ibid., pp. 84-87.

19. Arthur L. Wagner, *The Service of Security and Information*, 4th ed. (Kansas City: Hudson-Kimberly Co., 1896), p. 7.

20. Ibid., pp. 20-21.

21. Ibid. (1903 ed.), p. 34.

22. Arthur L. Wagner, *Organization and Tactics* (Kansas City: Hudson-Kimberly Co., 1895), p. 87.

23. Ibid., p. 105.

24. Ibid., pp. 131-36, 141, 145.

25. File 6144-ACP-1886, RG 94.

26. Comparison based on variety of data from respective personnel files 2908-ACP-1882 and 6144-ACP-1886, RG 94.

27. Eben Swift, "Memoranda," p. 118, Eben Swift Papers, U.S. Military Academy Library.

28. George Van Horn Moseley to Henry T. Allen, May 28, 1914, Miscellaneous General Staff Records, Record Group 165, National Archives.

29. Wagner, report, July 11, 1894, file 6144-ACP-1886, RG 94.

30. Eben Swift to William A. Ganoe, November 10, 1924, chapter notes vol. 5, box 16, John McAuley Palmer Papers, Library of Congress.

31. Eben Swift, *Orders* (Fort Leavenworth: Army Service Schools Press, 1906), pp. 3, 16, 21-22.

32. Eben Swift, *A Simplified War Game by General Verdy du Vernois* (Kansas City: Hudson-Kimberly Co., 1897), pp. 5, 7-9. For a description of the evolution of war games, see Farrand Sayre, *Map Maneuvers and Tactical Rides* (Fort Leavenworth: Army Service Schools Press, 1910), pp. 7-22.

33. Swift to Ganoe, November 10, 1924, chapter notes, vol. 5, box 16, Palmer Papers.

34. Hall to Swift, January 20, 1897, Eben Swift Papers, National Archives Gift Collection, RG 200, National Archives.

35. Report of the Commanding General, *Annual Reports of the War Department* (Washington, D.C.: GPO, 1892), 1: 58. This was the 1891 report.

36. William H. Carter, "The Infantry and Cavalry School," *Journal of the Military Service Institution* 15 (July 1894): 752.

37. Elmer W. Hubbard, "The Military Academy and the Education of Officers," *Journal of the Military Service Institution* 16 (January 1895): 20.

38. Adjutant General to Hawkins, December 14, 1896, file 47075, RG 94.

39. William Harding Carter, "The Greater Leavenworth," *Cavalry Journal* 25 (October 1914): 174.

40. James Pettit, "Comment and Criticisms: Reply to Wagner's Comments on 'Proper Military Education,'" *Journal of the Military Service Institution* 20 (May 1897): 632.

4

LEAVENWORTH
AND THE ELIHU
ROOT REFORMS

In April 1898 the War Department closed the Infantry and
Cavalry School and ordered students and instructors to their
regiments for service against Spain. The school did not reopen
until September 1, 1902. Events during the intervening four
years greatly affected the future development of Leavenworth
because the War Department made changes to improve the organization of the army, the structure of the educational system,
and the effectiveness of Leavenworth itself.

From all accounts, graduates of the pre-1898 school performed admirably in Cuba, Puerto Rico, and the Philippines.
Even a skeptic of educated soldiers like General Nelson A. Miles
acknowledged the valuable instruction officers had received at
the service school and the graduates' contribution to the American war effort.[1] Junior rank and small numbers, however, prevented graduates from influencing the conduct of the war beyond the tactical level. Because the Spanish-American War involved overseas, joint army-navy operations on at least three
fronts and the mobilization of state volunteers and militia, the
American war effort required more than the tactical ability
possessed by the Regulars.

The war exposed an inefficient means of mobilizing reserves,
an unworkable command structure at the highest level, and the

lack of a strategic planning agency. Organizational problems, not the quality of its troops and tactical leaders, hindered the army during the war. Elihu Root, appointed secretary of war in August 1899, recognized these weaknesses and with the assistance of able subordinates sought to rectify them. With no previous experience in military affairs, Root relied on others for information and ideas. He studied the Dodge Commission investigation of the War Department's failures during the war; corresponded with Colonel William Cary Sanger of the New York National Guard who was in Europe investigating European armies; and read Spenser Wilkinson's treatise, *The Brain of an Army*, which praised the German general staff and War College. William H. Carter, then assistant adjutant general, introduced the writings of Emory Upton to the secretary.[2] Root did not wholly accept Upton's concept of the proper military system for the United States but did rely on him for many details.[3] The officer who virtually ran the War Department in 1898, Adjutant General Henry C. Corbin, discussed army problems with Root. From his reading and discussions Root derived two fundamental propositions about the nature of the American military system: "that the real object of having an Army is to provide for war" and "that the regular establishment in the United States will probably never be by itself the whole machine with which any war will be fought."[4] His reform proposals followed from these two premises.

To correct the ills of 1898, Root fought for legislation that increased federal authority over the state militias, replaced the commanding general with a Chief of Staff, and established the General Staff. By creating the position of Chief of Staff to be the principal military adviser to the president and to issue orders in the name of the civilian authority, Root tried to strengthen the lines of authority and responsibility among the president, the secretary of war, and the army. The General Staff assisted the Chief of Staff with his duties by collecting military information, supervising the educational and other technical functions of the army, and planning for possible future military operations. Because few of the early general staff officers, and even Root himself, truly understood how the system should work, the effectiveness and impact of the War Department General Staff remained limited until World War I.

In the short run, the reserve, command, and planning aspects of the Root reforms were not a success. But they were an attempt at modernizing the army and solving its organizational problems. If they failed to do that, they nonetheless provided some basis for adjusting to these problems in the future. Root's restructuring of the army educational system was more successful.

Several of Root's associates at the War Department were strong proponents of postgraduate military education. William H. Carter, Root's closest adviser on the subject, advocated the systematic education of all officers. In 1902 he wrote that the "great and essential point" of postgraduate military education was to train all officers to react quickly and alertly in all emergencies.[5] Brigadier General Tasker Bliss, the first president of the Army War College, wrote to the secretary that officers needed to know more about their profession than just drill regulations and the Articles of War; military schools should provide this knowledge.[6] Others in the War Department wanted to educate junior officers in the planning, supply, and command problems they would face later in their careers. To accomplish this they wanted immediately to reopen and expand the service schools.[7] His experience gained while commanding American troops in China convinced General Adna Chaffee that "we are the most slouchy soldiers in the world." He wrote Root that discipline and particularly military instruction, at all levels, could overcome this.[8] Although some, including the commanding general, Nelson A. Miles, denigrated the value of military education, they did not sway Root.[9]

From 1899 until he left the War Department in 1904, the cause of military education remained central to Root's reforms. Like Sherman and Upton, he recognized the "rapid advance of military science" and consequently the growing importance of "thorough and broad education for military officers."[10] The service schools, particularly Leavenworth, impressed the secretary. According to him, although graduates had demonstrated high standards of individual excellence during the Spanish War

and activities thereafter, too few officers had had the benefits
of the schools. With Root's plans for other reforms and with
the expansion of the army in 1901, a system for educating officers became even more essential. In particular the proposed
General Staff needed specially trained officers.

The expansion of the army after the Spanish War initially
retarded efforts to establish postgraduate schools while simul-
taneously reinforcing the arguments in their favor. Because of
expansion by five cavalry and five infantry regiments and the
increased responsibilities in colonial administration, the army
could not spare officers either to teach or to learn. Thus Root
delayed reopening the schools until 1902.[11] Expansion also
brought a large number of young, untrained officers into the
army. In 1902 of 2,000 line officers, 1,818 had received commissions since the beginning of the war with Spain. Only 276
were West Point graduates. Another 414 were former enlisted
men, 616 were previously volunteer officers, and 512 had direct
commissions from civilian life. Nearly half of all officers of the
line and almost all the lieutenants of the line (1,542) had no
military education.[12] Root, striving for a systematic education
for all officers at all levels, wanted to eliminate the haphazard
and contradictory efforts to train officers that had existed in
the army before 1898. With the assistance of his subordinates,
particularly Carter, between 1900 and 1902 the secretary
planned and inaugurated a new system of military education.

Carter presented the objectives, noted the options, and
specified the means. The objective was a progressive system of
army schools to meet the changing educational requirements
as an officer progressed through his career. Each school would
concentrate on one level of military science—tactics, staff
functions, or strategy. As the curriculum at each level became
more difficult, the students became more adept. Theoretically
only the best graduates at one level could progress to the next
highest school. The War College, at the apex of the system,
would serve as an educational institution but would also supervise instruction at the lower-level schools. Below the War College were the General Service and Staff College at Leavenworth,
several special service schools for technical branches such as

the artillery, signal service, and engineers, and, at the lowest, post schools providing elementary military instruction.

Carter began with the premise that the lyceum system, then existing for instruction of junior officers, was "most unsatisfactory." He proposed to replace it with schools at each post offering instruction in the tactical and administrative duties required of lieutenants and that would prepare them for instruction at the service schools. Carter wanted a uniform system of instruction that did not depend on the interests and idiosyncrasies of individual post commanders. An explicit course of study for the post schools would ensure the uniformity previously lacking.[13]

War Department orders published in 1902 charged post commanders with the operation of the post schools, detailed field officers and captains with over ten years' service as instructors, and defined students as captains of the line with fewer than ten years of service and all lieutenants. Theoretical instruction consisted of ninety school days, two hours of recitation per day, between November and April. At the end of each term (the complete course of study at the post schools was two terms) a board of officers examined students in the subjects just completed. The examining board in conjunction with the instructors reported on the officers exhibiting the most "aptitude and intelligence" for consideration as students at Leavenworth and the other service schools.[14]

At the other end of Root's educational system was the Army War College, whose students were to be distinguished Leavenworth graduates and outstanding officers selected by the War Department. Bliss, the first War College president, believed the school should study strategic problems and also prepare the plans for mobilization, training, and movement of troops in time of war. He thought that those officers most likely to carry out American war plans should assemble periodically at the War College to study and revise them. Lectures by soldiers, diplomats, lawyers, and scholars and a large-scale war game would supplement their conferences. The War College as Bliss operated it would do staff work rather than function as a purely academic institution and thus act as an adjunct of the General Staff.[15]

The Army War College began its first year on November 1, 1903, but without students. General Bliss and his staff assisted the newly appointed and wholly inexperienced War Department General Staff and prepared a course of study for the students expected in the fall of 1904. Initially the course was unlike that of Leavenworth or other military schools. It had neither a specified length nor a required curriculum. Classes were small; the first had only nine students. In keeping with the ideas of its patrons, the War College stressed learning by doing, particularly in preparing war plans and conducting map exercises and war games involving the largest military units. During the years before World War I, the War College course gradually changed to become more and more like Leavenworth in its method of instruction as well as in content. By 1916 only its role in preparing war plans distinguished it from the Leavenworth Staff College.[16]

In Root's plans the special service schools and Leavenworth occupied a position between the post schools and the War College. He wanted to continue the Artillery School at Fort Monroe, the Cavalry and Light Artillery School at Fort Riley, the Engineer School of Application in Washington, and the School for Submarine Defense at Fort Totten, New York, as they had existed before the Spanish War. Within a few years the War Department added a Field Engineer School, a Signal School, and a Field Service and Correspondence School for Medical Officers at Fort Leavenworth to provide advanced training for promising officers within each branch. Some of the schools, particularly the one at Fort Riley, covered subjects also studied at Leavenworth, but essentially they were for branch specialists. For that reason graduates of the special service schools and the best students from the post schools could broaden their experience by attending Leavenworth.

To reflect the purpose of this institution more accurately, at Carter's insistence the War Department changed the name from the Infantry and Cavalry School to General Service and Staff College. As this designation indicated, the new Leavenworth was supposed to be a school for generalists, with emphasis on staff work. Training at the school was not for a single

branch "but for general utility in the administration and handling of higher commands of all arms."[17]

Carter, working closely with Root, arranged the curriculum
and set standards of qualification for students at the new institution. Despite other responsibilities, Root showed much interest
in Leavenworth and even read essays by former students.[18] Carter and the secretary realized that because the young, newly
commissioned officers had little previous military education, the
schools had to reopen as soon as possible.[19] In the long run they
believed an effective lyceum system would allow all service
schools to conduct advanced education. Leavenworth could become an educational center for the entire army where Regular
and militia officers prepared for the task of training and leading the short-service recruits in time of war.[20]

But the large influx of young, inexperienced officers and the
necessity of rapidly preparing them for their new responsibilities
continued to be a problem. To overcome this Carter recommended temporarily reducing the Leavenworth course to one
year.[21] Although diluting the quality of the curriculum, this
change allowed more officers to receive instruction. The War
Department orders that reopened Leavenworth encompassed
Carter's ideas on the scope and mission of the school.

On July 1, 1902, the War Department announced the school
would open September 1.[22] Brigadier General J. Franklin Bell
was to be the commandant, but duties in the Philippines de-
tained him for nearly a year. In his interim, despite the presence
of two successive acting commandants, Colonels Jacob A. Augur
and Charles W. Miner, the War College Board (functioning as a
provisional general staff) closely supervised the school. It selected
the first students from the lineal lists of cavalry and infantry
lieutenants. Because selection was by block, with no regard for
background or aptitude, the class was much less homogeneous
and much less prepared for the rigors of the course than were
the classes immediately before the Spanish War. Regrettably
this was the best way to be certain that the large group of recently commissioned cavalry and infantry officers received some
basic military education. All first lieutenants on the army list
senior to those selected were West Point graduates; no West

Pointers were in the first General Service and Staff College class. Although seventy-two of the ninety-five students received Regular Army commissions in 1901 and none had been officers before 1898, these men were not new recruits. All had seen active Regular or volunteer service during the Spanish War or Philippine insurrection. Unfortunately for some, their field service was insufficient preparation for the Leavenworth course. Only fourteen were college graduates. Failures and dropouts were greater in the first class after the Spanish War than in any other class between 1881 and 1916.[23]

A five-man board of officers, appointed by the War College Board, met July 21, 1902, to select instructors and "recommend a proper course of instruction." The final course of study was a compromise based on the premise that the one-year course was a temporary measure and a two-year course soon would be reinstituted. The course also included elementary instruction, which eventually would be taught at the post schools. Much of the advanced tactical and engineering instruction, which the board wanted to include, could not be part of the one-year course.[24]

A comparison of the 1902 course with the pre-1898 Leavenworth reveals significant differences. Students in 1902 did not have maneuvers and war games nor did they study logistics, military history, strategy, or ironically, staff duties, which prior to the Spanish War had been part of the Leavenworth curriculum. Subjects taught in the department of tactics were practically identical in 1897 and 1902: small arms firing regulations, infantry and cavalry drill regulations, equitation and hippology, manual of guard duty, troops in campaign, security and information, and organization and tactics. These were subjects basic to the education of junior officers. Despite some similarity in the subjects studied, the time devoted to them at the new school was more superficial and concentrated on more elementary military subjects than had that at the Infantry and Cavalry School.

On September 1 the course began with Major Smith S. Leach, the assistant commandant, delivering an opening address. Leach advised the students: "We are equally concerned with your present achievement and your future promise." The college would attempt to fit officers to duties they faced in their present grades and would designate students likely to become the best officers in higher grades.[25] Of the first day's activities the acting commandant reported to the War Department: "The General Service and Staff College opened yesterday with address by the Assistant Commandant, recitation in afternoon in engineering, everything in good shape and condition; regret to report 32 absentees."[26]

The students who did not report for the first day of classes in 1902 signaled the beginning of problems that hampered the General Service and Staff College during the ensuing two years. Unlike other difficulties, the problem of the tardy students solved itself. Pressing duties had delayed most of them in the Philippines. Eventually they all reported to Leavenworth.[27] Compared to other academic and administrative difficulties, the late arrivals were but a minor problem.

The results of the semiannual examination, held in January 1903, were so poor that *The Nation* claimed half the Leavenworth class had failed.[28] Although this report exaggerated the number of failures, the facts were bad enough. Forty-two students failed at least one of the six tests given by the department of tactics. Nearly one-third of those examined in the two basic tactics courses, security and information and small arms firing regulations, failed. A similar number did not pass the examination in topography, the elementary engineering course. Appalled but not surprised, the senior instructor in tactics wrote: "The handwriting of many of the papers is so poor as to be scarcely legible, and there is noticeable deficiency in orthography and grammar, while punctuation seems to be practically an unknown art."[29] Circumstances beyond the control of Leavenworth authorities—particularly lack of motivation on the part of some students and the inadequate educational backgrounds of many others—had created the situation.

For the eight students who had failed five or more subjects the faculty ordered reexaminations. Following the second series of exams all eight remained deficient in at least one subject. In the opinion of the commandant, two students had done their

best and failed only because of their poor elementary education. He criticized the other six for "lack of application" and
"indifference."[30] Because they failed in their professional ob-
ligations, the secretary of war brought charges against these
students. The eventual result was one conviction resulting in
dismissal from the service; three convictions resulting in loss
of files on the lineal seniority list, reprimands, and fines; one
resignation; and one acquittal. In June 1903, at the conclusion
of the course, thirteen students were deficient.[31]

Most of the personnel problems, which were the principal
cause of the poor performance of the class of 1902-03, had resulted from selecting that class en masse from the lineal list of
lieutenants with no regard for past performance or future potential. Pressures of army reorganization had forced this solution on the War College Board. To overcome these difficulties
and in keeping with the original intention of Secretary Root
and his educational advisers, the board requested regimental
commanders to recommend "promising officers" for the course
at the General Service and Staff College beginning September 1,
1903. During July the board and the secretary of war approved
those selected. The colonels making the recommendations most
often cited an officer's performance in the garrison schools as
the reason for selection. Officers who requested to go to the
school usually received the assignment.[32]

The class entering in 1903 generally was more experienced
than the 1902 class; students had been commissioned one or
two years earlier than the previous group. More officers in the
1903 class initially had received Regular Army commissions,
whereas nearly all of the 1902 class first had been Volunteer
officers. Finally, the class of 1903-04 included seven West
Pointers; there had been none the year before.[33] The appointment of these seven, though a small percentage of a class of over
ninety, meant that the War Department wanted Leavenworth to
become more than simply a remedial training academy.

At least in part the change in selection procedures accounted
for a radical change in the results of the semiannual exam in
December 1903, when only two students were deficient in tactics and three in engineering. Two were immediately reexamined

and passed, while the other three waited until the June exams when "they fully met the requirements of the college."[34] This was quite a contrast to the previous year.

The classroom procedures, teaching methods, and curriculum at the General Service and Staff College demonstrated that the course remained largely remedial and required improvements. A strict marking system, with grades carried to three decimal places, led to cramming and rote memorization of the assigned textbooks upon which final grades in every course were largely based. Students believed the more closely they adhered to the wording of the text, the higher would be their grade.[35] Proceedings within the classroom were equally rigid. Although the classroom decorum was more appropriate to a grammar than to a postgraduate school, similar procedures were then in vogue at West Point. The similarities were not entirely coincidental. Under more satisfactory circumstances, more of the students might have been West Pointers.[36]

Recitations and other assemblages of the class began with the instructor calling the roll. When any officer senior to the instructor entered the room, students came to attention. Conversation was prohibited. While reciting, students faced the instructor, not the class. They could glance at the blackboard and use wooden pointers to indicate on the blackboard matters under discussion. These pointers, when not used, were held "in the position of order arms of the saber."[37] Students were very critical of the instruction, which placed so much emphasis on memorization. Several believed that better methods, particularly in the tactical work, would have eliminated almost all discontent.[38]

The study of tactics dominated the General Service and Staff College curriculum; well over half of instruction time was allotted to that department. Lectures, recitations, and textbook readings on the subject were followed by a limited number of practical exercises. Because the department wanted to keep the instruction within the scope of the students' probable duties, the first year's course was little better than what Root and Carter had contemplated for the post schools.

The instruction in tactics began with a survey of the basics:

small arms firing regulations, manual of guard duty, infantry
drill regulations, and cavalry drill regulations. Commanding
units up to infantry battalion or cavalry squadron size at drill
and battle formation was the principal practical work in cavalry
and infantry drill regulations. One tactics instructor gave riding
lessons to prepare "the officer to appear before troops, mounted,
wearing saber and spur and prepared to take care of himself and
his horse."[39] At the heart of the curriculum were courses in
security and information and organization and tactics, based on
Wagner's two books. These were good, basic narratives but included none of the problem-solving situations then popular in
professional military literature, especially in Europe. During
the first year (1902-03) lectures, recitations on Wagner, and a
few simple field problems predominated. For the second class
(1903-04) the instructors added map problems, terrain walks,
and terrain rides to introduce tactical principles and simple
problem solving to young officers.

As a culmination to the tactical work for 1904, the department of tactics held a day-long war game, but insufficient time
prevented more extensive use of the war game technique for
tactical training. Because one objective of the school was to
point the way for further self-instruction and for the instruction of others, the staff believed this limited exposure to war
gaming was adequate.[40]

According to regulations, theoretical work in the department of tactics concluded with an elementary course in strategy.
Lack of time and the poor preparation of the students for such
a course necessitated eliminating it the opening year. During
the second year the strategy course consisted of lectures prepared by Colonel Wagner, quizzes, and a written examination.
The first and last lectures in the series were on the principles
of strategy and their application. Other lectures covered the
strategy of the Napoleonic wars, the Civil War, the Franco-
Prussian War, and two lesser nineteenth-century European
wars. Future instructors would expand this cursory examination of strategy to a more prominent place in the curriculum.

The remainder of the course at the General Service and
Staff College consisted of engineering, law, and military sanita-

tion and hygiene. Instruction in all three further emphasized that from 1902 to 1904 Leavenworth was preparing previously unschooled junior officers in basic military subjects. For instance, in engineering, besides learning to read and sketch maps, the students actually dug trenches, strung barbed wire, and built fieldworks in connection with the course on field fortifications. Students were learning by doing, but much of the work would lose its significance over the course of an officer's career. In contrast lectures, readings, and recitations were the only means of instruction in law and military sanitation and hygiene courses. Instructors in all departments were unsatisfied with the results obtained during the first two academic years, and they looked forward to expected changes in the future.

The years from 1902 to 1904 were a time of transition for Leavenworth and a period in which it had to attempt often conflicting tasks. First, it had to meet the immediate needs of an expanded army by providing remedial military instruction for recently commissioned officers. But it also attempted to prepare the basis for an expanded role for itself in educating experienced company and field grade line and staff officers as envisaged by Root and Carter. The school was in a state of becoming an important cog in the army's educational system. Its potential had yet to be achieved.

NOTES

1. Report of the Commanding General, *Annual Reports of the War Department* (Washington, D.C.: GPO., 1900), 1: 7.

2. General discussions of Secretary Root and his reforms include Walter Millis, *Arms and Men* (New York: G. P. Putnam's Sons, 1956), chap. 3; Otto L. Nelson, *National Security and the General Staff* (Washington, D.C.: Infantry Journal Press, 1946), chap. 3; Russell F. Weigley, *History of the United States Army* (New York: Macmillan, 1967), chap.14.

3. Root quoted in Philip C. Jessup, *Elihu Root; vol. 1: 1845-1909* (New York: Dodd, Mead, and Co., 1938), p. 242.

4. Report of the Secretary of War, *Annual Reports of the War Department* (Washington, D.C.: GPO., 1899), 1: 45-46.

5. William Harding Carter, "Postgraduate Instruction in the Army"

Educational Review 24 (December 1902): 438.

6. Bliss to Root, August 3, 1903, quoted in Frederick Palmer, *Bliss, Peacemaker* (New York: Dodd, Mead, and Co., 1934), p. 80.

7. Sharpe to Inspector General, June 30, 1901, file 401254, Record Group 94, National Archives.

8. Chaffee to Root, April 16, 1901, general correspondence, box 15, Elihu Root Papers, Library of Congress.

9. Root wrote Benjamin I. Wheeler, president of the University of California, that General Miles opposed the order establishing the Army War College and reopening the service schools. But Root noted that Miles's opinions "were not seriously entertained." Root to Wheeler, December 10, 1901. General correspondence, box 10, Root Papers.

10. Report of the Secretary of War, *Annual Reports of the War Department* (Washington, D.C.: GPO, 1901), 1: 20-21.

11. Ibid. (1900), 1: 49.

12. Ibid. (1903), 1: 30. This was the report for 1902.

13. Carter to Adjutant General, May 25, 1901, quoted in William Harding Carter, *Creation of the American General Staff*, S. Doc. 119, 68th Cong., 1st sess., 1924, p. 5.

14. General Orders No. 102, War Department, September 22, 1902.

15. Report of the Army War College, *Annual Reports of the War Department* (Washington, D.C.: GPO, 1903), 4: 95-97.

16. George S. Pappas, *Prudens Futuri: The U. S. Army War College, 1901-1967* (Carlisle, Pa.: Alumni Association Army War College, 1967), pp. 37-40, chap. 4.

There were several reasons for these changes. Because the War Department General Staff and its adjunct, the Army War College, were not as involved in strategic planning as originally anticipated, there was less of an immediate need for the college to teach strategic subjects. Because many officers selected for the War College were not Leavenworth graduates, the college had to provide instruction in logistics, General Staff procedures, and even tactics, which were included in the Leavenworth program. Finally it was easier and more expedient to present narrow, professional courses than it was to cover subjects such as international relations, economics, industrial mobilization, and grand strategy.

17. *Annual Reports* (1903), p. 94.

18. William H. Carter, "The Greater Leavenworth," *Cavalry Journal* 25 (October 1914): 178, 189.

19. Carter to Adjutant General, December 30, 1899, quoted in ibid., p. 175.

20. Carter to Root, October 14, 1901, quoted in Carter, *General Staff*, p. 10.

21. Carter, memo on instruction in the Regular Army, n.d., quoted in ibid., p. 7.

22. General Orders No. 64, War Department, July 1, 1902.

23. Smith S. Leach, "Address on Opening of the General Service and Staff College," *Cavalry Journal* 12 (October 1902): 221; S. B. M. Young to Adjutant General, July 11, 1902, file 444633, RG 94.

24. Proceedings of a Board of Officers, July 21, 1902, file 444632/H, RG 94.

25. Leach, "Address," p. 220.

26. Col. Jacob A. Augur to Adjutant General, September 2, 1902, file 450608, RG 94.

27. Adjutant General to Commandant, September 8, 1902, file 450608/B, RG 94.

28. "Staff Problems," *Nation* 76 (April 9, 1903): 206.

29. Report on the Semi-Annual Examination, January 2, 1903, file 469189, RG 94.

30. Miner to Adjutant General, March 18, 1903, file 469189/B, RG 94.

31. Staff memo, September 10, 1903, file 643, RG 393.

32. War College Board to Adjutant General, April 17, 1903; War College Board to Adjutant General, July 17, 1903; Recommendations for General Service and Staff College, 1903-04, file 481454, RG 94.

33. Statistics are from the 1902 and 1903 *Official Army Register.*

34. "Annual Report of the Commandant," 1904, RG 94. Unless otherwise noted, all further citations to Leavenworth annual reports are to reports filed in Annual Report Box, for a particular year, Adjutant General Document File, RG 94. Through 1908 the Leavenworth annual reports were also published with *Annual Reports of the War Department.* After that year Leavenworth received only brief mention in the published reports.

35. Ewing E. Booth, *My Observations and Experiences in the U. S. Army* (Los Angeles, 1944), pp. 87-88.

36. For an excellent discussion of West Point education, see Roger H. Nye, "The United States Military Academy in an Era of Educational Reform, 1900-1925," (Ph.D. diss., Columbia University, 1968).

37. "The General Service and Staff College," *Cavalry Journal* 15 (October 1904): 360.

38. Capt. W. H. Oury to Secretary, September 30, 1906, file 5341, Army Service Schools File, 1901-18, Record Group 393, National Archives.

39. Tactics Report (Dickman), in 1903 annual report, RG 94.

40. "General Service and Staff College," p. 382.

5

GENERAL BELL AND THE NEW LEAVENWORTH

In the year after the opening of the General Service and Staff College, the faculty and staff made numerous recommendations for change. Until Brigadier General J. Franklin Bell arrived at Leavenworth, however, little was done. To some extent this was a matter of circumstance. Bell arrived at the end of the academic year when the War Department was most likely to approve changes. Furthermore the general orders that established the General Service and Staff College contemplated periodically revising the course and in fact anticipated eventually extending the course from one year to two. But Bell was the catalyst who effected the changes that shaped the schools until World War I.

General Bell had an unusual military career. He graduated from the United States Military Academy in 1878 and was still a lieutenant twenty years later. Only eight years after that, he was a major general and Chief of Staff of the army. Bell spent four years in the Philippines, where he gained a reputation as a brutal but militarily effective suppressor of insurrectionists, three years as commandant of Leavenworth, and then four years as Chief of Staff. (The army remembered Bell especially for his contribution to the schools. Today Bell Hall is the main academic building at the Command and General Staff College.)

Bell's interest in military education developed during the 1890s when he was regimental adjutant of the Seventh Cavalry stationed at Fort Riley, home of the Cavalry and Light Artillery School. Later, as school adjutant, he arranged class schedules, prepared problems in minor tactics, and helped administer the program of instruction. These activities broadened his military horizons and provided a field for study and reflection. Field service in the Philippines enhanced his reputation and experience. The Medal of Honor Bell won there was testament to the fact he was not simply a "book" soldier.[1]

During 1902 Secretary Root and Major General S. B. M. Young, president of the War College Board, considered several candidates for commandant. Two officers declined the job.[2] Bell's record and past interest in military schooling were important determinants in his appointment. Colonel Charles Miner, who was nearing retirement, administered the school for the first year after the reopening. It was clear, however, that he was little more than a caretaker until Bell arrived from the Philippines.

Unlike Miner, Bell was intellectually and personally committed to the task. A vigorous, extroverted, enthusiastic personality helped him convey to younger officers the importance of military education and the role Leavenworth could play as a catalyst for improving the army. The students liked the commandant. He participated with them in sports and addressed them and their wives by first names. In turn the students considered the commandant's wife sociable and "brainy."[3] But Bell did not allow familiarity with students to interfere with his drive to improve the school. His style of leadership was only more subtle than the autocracy practiced by most Old Army officers. By his actions and attitudes Bell inspired both faculty and students.

At the end of Bell's first year as commandant, the inspector general of the army visited Leavenworth and reported how General Bell had transformed the school:

All of the earnestness of his nature is in his work. He practically lives in the school building where his time is

devoted to thinking and formulating plans to elevate the
academic course. He goes among the students in the lyceum, talks with them, advises them, and inspires them
toward higher ideals. He follows them in their field work,
encourages them by his presence and impresses them with
his industry and perseverance.[4]

On July 31, 1903, shortly after he reported to Leavenworth,
Bell prepared a memorandum for the War College Board that
provided the intellectual justification as well as the practical
details for change. Not all the ideas in his report were original.
Before going to Kansas, he had conferred in Washington with
officers at the War Department who made suggestions on the
needs and organization of the school. Miner had also made recommendations in his annual report. The two commandants discussed the problems of the first year and agreed reforms were
needed. Because Miner was retiring, Bell had the job of proposing, lobbying for, and implementing the changes.

The continuing emphasis on practical application during the
previous twenty years' history of Leavenworth education greatly impressed Bell. Because he thought that the General Service
and Staff College had cut too many corners and had neglected
practical work during 1902 and 1903, he concluded: "The
more I consider the work done in the past, the more I am
impressed with the conviction that the school had attained a
high state of efficiency when temporarily suspended in 1898 by
the war with Spain. . . . Our first effort should be to get back,
as soon as possible, to the conditions then existing, with a view
to making further progress as additional experience and opportunity may permit." Bell proposed a number of temporary
changes, effective in September 1903, to permit a reexamina-
tion of the curriculum during the next year as the basis for future permanent changes. More importantly he recommended
returning to a two-year course beginning in September 1904 to
permit additional practical work and a more advanced curriculum. The 1902-03 year had demonstrated the shortcomings of
a single-year course in which instructors had to limit the number of practical exercises, discussions, and critiques. Bell realized

that insufficient time had forced the adoption of other expedients, "all tending to reduce the thoroughness and efficiency of instruction."

Rather than have one class of approximately a hundred officers attend the school for a two-year course, Bell recommended two classes, each with about fifty officers, pursuing the first and second year's courses, respectively, at the same time. Second-year students could assist the faculty by umpiring field problems, providing after-hours remedial help to those needing it, and conducting recitation sessions. Bell believed this system would benefit the first class by exposing them to the better members of the preceding class; it would benefit the advanced students by forcing them to study in depth the subjects they assisted in instructing; it would benefit instructors by relieving them from some of their teaching burden; and, importantly, it would benefit the army because fewer officers would have to be detatched as instructors from already shorthanded regiments.

Bell considered practical work "the most important part of the course." Map problems, tactical rides, and practice in writing orders were essential building blocks for tactical knowledge. Despite the value of written tactical exercises and exercises without troops, Bell thought the most valuable instruction for young officers was exercises with troops. Students commanding units much larger than they normally would in the course of their duties gained confidence and skill. But too often permanent garrisons lacked troops for extensive field maneuvers. Thus gradually the hard realities of troop shortages in the peacetime army led Bell to modify his views and turn to the applicatory method as means of furnishing young officers with troop leading experience.[5]

In a memorandum of July 31, 1903, Bell outlined many of the specific regulations that went into effect when the schools opened for the 1904-05 academic year. Additional work by Leavenworth and War Department officials was required to refine and implement these proposals. Colonel Arthur L. Wagner, after January 1904 the chief of the Third Division of the General Staff, was particularly active in formulating plans for change. Wagner was interested, experienced, and well placed.

During the year between July 1903 and September 1904, the Third Division considered the proposals for reform, modified them, and eventually prepared new school regulations. To assist these efforts, Bell visited Washington twice to consult the General Staff, the Chief of Staff, and the secretary of war. One member of the Third Division visited Leavenworth in the spring of 1904 and continued the exchange of views by talking with students, instructors, and staff. By May, when plans for reform had become well defined, Wagner prepared a draft general order, completely revising the organization and curriculum at Leavenworth, in which he reviewed the army educational system with the intent of better integrating the several schools into a consistent scheme.

The salient feature was the return to a two-year course, an idea the Third Division had adopted from Bell. But the division added staggered classes with a new group of students beginning each year. Only the best students from the first year would continue the second year. Leavenworth thus became two complete and separate schools: the Infantry and Cavalry School for the highest graduates of the garrison schools and the Army Staff College for the honor and distinguished graduates of the Infantry and Cavalry School.

Unlike past attempts at reform, the draft general orders represented a sharp break with the previous course of study. Instructors at the Infantry and Cavalry School would concentrate on practical work in the study of tactics, while strategy and military history became a more important part of the curriculum. Engineering would provide line officers valuable information applicable to duties in the field. Instruction in law grew to include criminal law, laws of evidence, and moot courts. Because of the army's overseas responsibilities in former Spanish possessions, the Third Division included Spanish as part of the curriculum.

The Staff College posed different problems. The Third Division wanted it to educate general staff officers and bridge the gap between the tactical experts from the Infantry and Cavalry School and the strategists from the War College. The course in military art would include lectures and recitations on general staff duties, original research in strategy and military history, written exercises in logistics, lectures on naval warfare, studies in military geography, instruction in grand tactics, and practical campaign studies based on visits to Civil War battlefields. Staff College students would prepare, umpire, and criticize problems in minor tactics at the Infantry and Cavalry School. In engineering the Staff College studied at a more advanced level subjects previously covered in the first year.[6]

While the General Staff pondered changes in organization and curriculum, Bell attempted to recruit instructors who could meet the greater demands of the new school. His initial effort was to lure Major Eben Swift from the adjutant general's office back to Leavenworth, where he had taught in the 1890s. Bell wanted "the very best talent in the Army" and therefore offered Swift the important military art department and eventual responsibility as assistant commandant. Delighted and flattered, Swift immediately accepted. But Bell had a more difficult time convincing the War Department he needed Swift. The Chief of Staff, Lieutenant General Adna R. Chaffee, objected to Swift's detail because of his past association with Leavenworth. Chaffee did not want a Leavenworth-based clique, or "closed corporation," to develop.[7]

Bell was concerned and wrote Chaffee explaining why he needed Swift. Military art was the most important department at the school; it required an officer who would command the complete respect of the students and have the characteristics of prestige, character, poise, and knowledge. The instructor had to "be able to cite with certainty numerous authoritative examples in support of his contentions in order to satisfy these bright young men that his opinion is correct and worthy of respect." According to Bell, Swift met all these prerequisites; indeed he was one of only a handful who did. Other officers could become qualified, but Swift already was.[8] After delaying a month, Chaffee approved; on May 2, 1904, Swift received orders to the school. The fight for Swift's services was indicative of future struggles to acquire and retain good instructors. Because qualified officers were in great demand throughout the army, Leavenworth's needs had to be weighed against those of the rest of the service. In September 1904 the faculty was better qualified than during the previous two years; all served with Bell's approval.

The students entering Leavenworth in the fall of 1904 were also of a higher quality than those of previous classes. At the graduation ceremonies for the General Service and Staff College, Bell announced that the fifteen highest graduates would attend the new Staff College. The chief of artillery selected three recent Artillery School graduates to represent that branch, and engineers picked two captains. Bell selected the remaining three Staff College students from the 1903 honor graduates of the General Staff Service and Staff College.[9] Because all others in that class were denied a second year of instruction, selection to the Staff College was a real opportunity for the 1903 honor graduates, Captain Ewing E. Booth, and Lieutenants Herbert J. Brees and Charles S. Haight.

According to regulations, the Infantry and Cavalry School students would be "one officer of not less than four years' service, nor above the rank of Captain, from each regiment of cavalry and infantry serving within the continental limits of the United States."[10] Aptitude, professional potential, and proficiency in the garrison school course were the criteria considered in making the selections. Regimental commanders selected a principal and an alternate. From this group the Chief of Staff made the final choice.

In September 1904 the revised organization and course of study at Leavenworth were complete. The commandant had selected the instructors he wanted; the army had sent promising officers there as students; and unlike earlier reforms, the two schools now had a definite role to fulfill within a system of officer education. From 1904 until the schools closed during World War I, the basic organization of the Leavenworth schools remained unchanged. The reforms Bell accomplished continued in effect.

The School of the Line (the new name given to the Infantry and Cavalry School in 1907) and the Army Staff College were the heart of the Leavenworth schools. When officers spoke of Leavenworth men, they meant graduates of one or both of these institutions. During these years, however, the army established other schools at the fort. By 1916 the Army Service Schools, the designation of all schools at Fort Leavenworth, included the Staff College, the School of the Line, the Signal School (established in 1904), and the Field Engineer School (established in 1910). Each had its own commandant, faculty, students, curriculum, and regulations. The commandant of the Staff College was also commandant of the Army Service Schools and coordinated the activities of all four schools in their use of the same facilities and instructors and in their joint field exercises; he also supervised the Staff College students who helped with instruction at the other schools. All four institutions contributed to the increased professionalization of the officer corps. Because they dealt with technical subjects and had far fewer graduates, the impact of the Signal School and Field Engineer School was limited. The Staff College and School of the Line, much broader in their professional appeal, presented a course of study relevant to officers of all arms.

Authorities at Leavenworth perceived their role as twofold. The Army Service Schools exposed staff and line officers to the organization, requirements, and function of all branches of the army. General Bell wanted to enlarge the schools and develop "a quasi-military university for the special education of all officers from practically all the departments of the army." He was unable to create a university, but Leavenworth went far toward fostering cooperation between the staff and the line and among the several branches. Second, Leavenworth officials wanted to develop individual officers capable of performing either staff or line duties. Bell hoped to arouse "the divine spirit of achievement, the noble art of getting things done."[11] Although military intellectuals had their place, Leavenworth men would be problem solvers imbued with common sense, not intellectual facileness.

To meet these goals the faculty constantly altered the curriculum and instruction methods. Questions such as how to grade students in practical fieldwork and whether to post class standings received much attention. Bell's 1906 annual report,

for instance, discussed at length the advisability of daily marking and public display of grades. School regulations on these
subjects continually changed. Curriculum and course content
also changed as the garrison schools improved and the ability of
students and instructors and the needs of the service changed.
Despite difficulties and many changes, the Leavenworth faculty
and War Department observers were eloquent in their praise of
the School of the Line and Staff College.

Because Leavenworth's past reputation as a "kindergarten"
haunted them, their present performance and image concerned
the faculty. At the opening ceremonies in 1904, Eben Swift declared the "kindergarten" was gone, replaced by a modern military school.[12] During the next few years Bell reiterated the
theme. Regardless of his reputation as a tactician, Bell claimed
he would have been a better officer and army educator had he
graduated from Leavenworth.[13] Outside observers were equally
impressed. Inspectors from Washington used terms such as "rapid
and marked" progress, "splendid work," "excellent results,"
"well managed departments," and "competent and efficient" instructors to describe conditions at the schools.[14] By World War
I Leavenworth had fulfilled the expectations that Root, Bell,
Swift, and the others held for it. The comment of Major General
Leonard Wood, the Chief of Staff, on the performance of the
schools in 1913 aptly fit what a professional military school
should accomplish: "They are teaching a sound doctrine and
our officers are commencing to speak a common language in a
military sense and to understand better the interdependence of
the different arms."[15]

Students had a somewhat different perspective. Particularly
during the Bell years many felt a great dynamism connected
with significant and meaningful change. George C. Marshall,
who reported to the post a few months after Bell had left, recalled: "The time I was at Leavenworth it was going through
a considerable change. They were in a sense finding themselves."
The permanent staff was indeed learning all the time. Emphasis
in practical work increased, more difficult courses were added,
and Leavenworth's reputation rose. Because he remained for
two years as an instructor, Marshall saw both sides of the

changes. He recognized that progress, in the form of "very fine technique," emerged from mistakes, reevaluations, and hard work.[16] A sometime critic of Leavenworth, Lieutenant Colonel Robert L. Bullard, attended a short course at the schools in 1911. At that time the activity of the schools impressed even him: "Find this a great post, greater than ever and all intent on military instruction. One catches the hum, the spirit, the contagion before he knows it."[17]

Leavenworth was changing, but so was the army, and people at the schools recognized the connection between these changes. According to one graduate, Royden C. Beebe, a contemporary of Marshall, General Bell often discussed these transformations with the students.[18] Another of Marshall's classmates, Fay Brabson, made the connection in a slightly different manner. He defined military professionalism as "talking the same language" as fellow officers. Brabson thought the schools inculcated exactly that: "You knew what another Leavenworth man was talking about."[19]

Bell's contributions to these developments were several and varied. Initially he acted as an interpreter and implementer of the plans for reform that Root and Carter had originated. As an organizer and administrator, he brought about modifications in those plans and established the solid organizational base on which Leavenworth would build after he had departed. Although he was not principally a teacher, Bell occasionally led classes, particularly on terrain rides, where his instructional methods, tactical knowledge, and easy manner found a receptive audience among the students.[20] Bell's efforts added a spirit and sense of purpose to students and instructors and immeasurably raised the morale and collective self-esteem of the schools.

Perhaps Bell's greatest contribution, as commandant and then as Chief of Staff, was to try to make postgraduate military education, particularly Leavenworth education, respectable in the eyes of the Old Army. To younger officers Bell made clear that graduation from Leavenworth would benefit professional development and advancement. One officer recalled: "It had been rumored through the army that if any officer expected or wanted high command in war he had better graduate from both schools.

General J. Franklin Bell was supposed to be the author of that rumor."[21]

Bell actively recruited promising young officers to attend Leavenworth, which occasionally took considerable time. Captain George Van Horn Moseley applied for Leavenworth over a year after Bell, through the school secretary, Captain Milton F. Davis, and Moseley's commanding officer, General Jesse M. Lee, began his effort to recruit the young officer. Davis wrote Moseley in February 1906: "Beginning about five years from the present time, the best graduates . . . will be marked men and will be in line for choice of all kinds of select details through the service." Countering Moseley's inclination to remain with his regiment, Davis maintained that regimental duty was necessary but an officer's reputation was made "away from the colors."[22] Both Davis and Lee reminded Moseley that Bell would soon become Chief of Staff, probably would remain at the head of the army for several years, and would boost the careers of young, able officers on whom he had his eye.[23] Leavenworth was then the easiest way to catch Bell's eye. Finally, in March 1907, Moseley sought his regiment's detail for Leavenworth and was accepted.

Even more difficult to convince were the older, senior officers, especially the regimental commanders, to whom the idea of education for soldiers was anathema. Because they selected candidates for Leavenworth, administered the post schools, and could influence their subordinates positively or negatively regarding military education, it was important to overcome the innate skepticism of this group. Nearly all of the forty-five cavalry and infantry regimental commanders in 1904 had been commissioned during or shortly after the Civil War, only nineteen were West Point graduates, and only two had attended any postgraduate school. Soldiers from that era regarded army officers as heroic leaders, were more than slightly anti-intellectual, and considered reading, writing, and arithmetic sufficient education for officers. They had not assimilated the technological, tactical, and organizational changes then taking place in warfare nor did they recognize the role of the military manager—a role Leavenworth was preparing officers to assume. Because Bell was clearly in the mold of a heroic leader, his policies regarding education were somewhat more palatable for these older officers. As Chief of Staff he gave preferential treatment to field grade officers over company grade officers in appointing them to the service schools or the War College or the General Staff. He believed first-hand experience with postgraduate military education would convince them of its benefits and gain their support for the system. Over time this evolution took place, but not without difficulty. Simple attrition was partly responsible, but Bell did change some attitudes. By 1909 only one Civil War veteran remained as one of the forty-five regimental commanders (two of whom had attended a postgraduate school and thirty-three of whom were West Pointers). In 1914 there were no Civil War veterans left, West Pointers increased to thirty-eight, and, significantly, ten of the regimental commanders had gone to a postgraduate school (nine to the Army War College).[24]

Though not single-handedly, Bell had convinced numerous junior officers to attend the service schools and had convinced senior officers of the benefits of military education. As commandant he instilled a pride and esprit at Leavenworth that came to mark Leavenworth men. As Chief of Staff he ensured that the schools flourished and grew. After World War I General Pershing acknowledged this effort: "Despite persistent and powerful opposition in and out of the Army, General Bell, while Chief of Staff, had succeeded in developing through our service schools an effective system of training a limited number of officers for command and staff duty and for this contribution to our success he deserves the highest praise."[25]

NOTES

1. Edgar Frank Raines, Jr., "The Early Career of Major General James Franklin Bell, USA, 1856-1903" (Master's thesis, Southern Illinois University, 1968); Edgar Frank Raines, Jr., "Major General J. Franklin Bell

and Military Reform: The Chief of Staff Years, 1906-1910" (Ph.D. diss., University of Wisconsin, 1976).

2. Young to Root, December 23, 1901, file 414805, Record Group 94, National Archives. The other officers considered were Brigadier General William A. Kobbe and Major William P. Duvall.

3. Forrest C. Pogue interviews with Royden Beebe, April 6, 1961, and Charles D. Herron, May 28, 1958; also Forrest C. Pogue, *George C. Marshall: Education of a General* (New York: Viking Press, 1963), p. 95.

4. Brig. Gen. G. H. Burton, extract from report, November 18, 1904, file 685, RG 393.

5. Bell to War College Board, July 31, 1903, file 525015, RG 94.

6. Memo report no. 73, May 18, 1904, Third Division General Staff, RG 165.

7. Bell to Swift, February 26, 1904; Swift to Bell, March 4, 1904; Chaffee to Bell, March 22, 1904: file 2145, RG 393.

8. Bell to Chaffee, March 24, 25, 1904, file 2145, RG 393.

9. Memo report no. 101, June 29, 1904, memo report no. 114, July 20, 1903, Third Division General Staff, RG 165.

10. General orders no. 115, War Department, June 27, 1904. The regulations governing admission periodically changed. Although most graduates from 1904 to 1916 were captains, some lieutenants and a few majors also attended. Branch participation also broadened to include engineers, artillerymen, and officers from support services. See appendixes 2 and 3 for statistics on Leavenworth students.

11. Bell quoted in Henry Shindler and E. E. Booth, *History of the Army Service Schools* (Fort Leavenworth: Army Service Schools Press, 1908), p. iv.

12. Eben Swift, *Remarks Introductory to the Course in Military Art, 1904* (Fort Leavenworth: Army Service Schools Press, 1904), p. 1.

13. Bell to Adjutant General, March 16, 1905, file 990754, RG 94.

14. Report of the Inspector General, *Annual Reports of the War Department* (Washington, D.C.: GPO, 1905), 1: 450; report of Colonel J. L. Chamberlain, May 21-4, 1906, file 4407, RG 393; report of Colonel F. K. Ward, May 13, 1907, quoted in Annual Report of the Commandant, 1907, RG 94.

15. Report of the Chief of Staff, *Annual Reports of the War Department* (Washington, D.C.: GPO, 1913), 1: 177.

16. Forrest C. Pogue interview with George C. Marshall, April 4, 1957.

17. Robert L. Bullard, January 11, 1911, diary book 5, Robert L. Bullard Papers, Library of Congress.

18. Pogue interview with Beebe, April 6, 1961.

19. Author interview with Fay Brabson, January 10, 1970.

20. Lieutenant W. N. Hughes to Secretary, May 20, 1905, file 1260, RG 393.

21. L. M. Nuttman to author, December 16, 1971.

22. Davis to Moseley, February 8, 1906, scrapbook (1889-1911), George Van Horn Moseley Papers, Library of Congress.

23. Lee to Moseley, April 7, 1907, Scrapbook, Moseley Papers.

24. Statistics compiled from 1904, 1909, and 1914 *Army Registers.*

25. John J. Pershing, *My Experiences in the World War* (New York: Frederick A. Stokes Co., 1931), 1: 41.

6

LINE SCHOOL,
STAFF COLLEGE,
AND LEAVENWORTH
DOCTRINE

Between the Spanish-American War and World War I the American army was small compared to those of other major powers,
was scattered at posts (which varied in size from company to
brigade) from Governor's Island to Manila, and was often not
equipped with the most modern arms and munitions. Its tactical
units were understrength, sometimes with enlistments lagging,
desertions high, and officers away on detail. Despite such hardships these years marked a renaissance in the study of military
art within the army. A few American pioneers, like Emory
Upton, John Bigelow, and Arthur Wagner, had written books
on tactics and strategy in the late nineteenth century, and some
American officers had studied European tactical works. But the
first years of the new century witnessed a proliferation of American-authored books and articles on tactics and strategy, as well
as an abundance of English translations of foreign military
works. Instructors and students at the Leavenworth schools
wrote and translated many of these studies, and the Leavenworth faculty adapted the applicatory method to the study of
tactics in the U. S. Army.

The interest in tactics was not limited to the schools, though
they were certainly central to this revival. The professional mili-

tary journals published numerous articles on strategy, tactics, and military history by authors who ranged from junior second lieutenants to experienced generals. Throughout the army's educational system, from the garrison schools to the War College, tactics was an essential part of the curriculum. Finally, more than any other factor, an officer's professional reputation rested on his ability as a tactician. Men such as John J. Pershing and James G. Harbord gained reputations for their tactical prowess fighting insurrectos and Moros in the Philippines. Others, including young officers like George C. Marshall and more experienced men like Hunter Liggett, built reputations based on the tactical knowledge they exhibited in the schools and maneuvers of the peacetime army.

Tactics was but part of a broader field described during these years as military art, which included study of strategy, general staff duties, logistics, weapons, and military history. American experience in the Spanish War and the Philippines and foreign experience in the Franco-Prussian War, the Boer War, and the Russo-Japanese War demonstrated the changing nature of warfare and the importance of these subjects. The newly established War Department General Staff created a need for officers trained in staff duties. At Leavenworth the study of military art attempted to fill these needs.

Past experience formed the basis of military education, particularly of tactical instruction. Military educators believed their task was to study, analyze, and convert to the profit and use of the army the recent wartime experiences. As one Leavenworth instructor put it: "We cannot organize war for the purpose of instruction. We must imagine it and simulate it."[1] By keeping abreast of military developments in other countries and continually examining its own tactical doctrine, the army tried to avoid adapting outdated tactics based totally on past performance. Unless the nation wanted to rely on the innate military genius of its citizens, the army had no alternative to studying the past in light of current developments.

Military educators were skeptical of military genius. They believed that untrained amateur commanders, no matter how well endowed with innate ability, had little chance against a trained army commanded by educated professionals. Technical knowledge and tactical ability, attained through experience and study, were essential to military success. Instruction at the schools would assist officers in developing their analytical, decision-making, and tactical ability. Instruction would not stifle initiative and self-reliance or bind officers to a rigid system. On the other hand, the army wanted an officer corps with good general ability rather than a few brilliant officers and the rest "fodder for elimination boards."[2]

The goal was to produce "safe" leaders. Military operations required teamwork based on mutual understanding among commanders and subordinates. To produce officers capable of cooperation in time of stress required, within reason, uniformity of thought, uniformity of methods, and uniformity of doctrine. Officers from exactly the same mold, who in a given situation would do precisely as their peers, were not wanted. The army did want a similarity in approaching and understanding tactical problems. Radical departures from what superiors and subordinates expected could prove fatal in combat. Thus military educators wanted officers who thought similarly, not identically.

Solving practical problems was central to exercising command of any military unit from a platoon to a field army. It was on his ability to solve problems that an officer's tactical reputation rested. Because few officers would admit shortcomings as tacticians, the task of the military educators was difficult. As one Leavenworth instructor put it: "Every officer has professional pride. He may be indolent. He may be somewhat deficient in energy and ambition. He may even confess his ignorance of ration tables, guardhouse regulations, typhoid germs, and such like nightmares of military genius; but he will be a rare bird and a lonesome one if he confesses his inferiority as a tactician." At Leavenworth students would admit their inability to master Spanish and their lack of talent as mapmakers, but they blamed any mistakes or criticisms of their solutions of tactical problems on the "capricious and perverted views of a demented instructor."[3]

Tactics, the art of maneuvering troops on the battlefield, and grand tactics, the handling of armies in battle, were the heart of the Leavenworth curriculum. The School of the Line instructed officers in proper methods of troop leading and care of troops in wartime and in the training of troops in peacetime. The course, building on what officers had already learned at the garrison schools, emphasized operations of regiments, brigades, and divisions in offensive and defensive combat. Students solved numerous and progressively more difficult practical problems during their ten months of instruction, in which they learned duties as tactical commanders. At the Staff College the practical problems were more difficult and included operations of army corps, with particular emphasis on the duties of general staff officers.

Although most students considered the Staff College more prestigious than the School of the Line, over a period of years the faculty at Leavenworth stressed the mission of the school over that of the college. One commandant stated he would sacrifice the interests of "any or all" of the other service schools to that of the School of the Line because it was "the most important educational agency for the promotion of efficiency of the army."[4] Authorities at Leavenworth wanted to maintain the maximum number of line students. The army needed only a few staff officers but many well-trained line officers. A major factor behind this belief in the supremacy of the School of the Line was the developing quality of the military art department, which most officers considered "the only really important one [academic department] in the whole school."[5]

Only half of the students of the first-year class were selected for the Staff course, so competition was intense and students considered admission a real honor. If graduates of the School of the Line were professionalized there, Staff College graduates were those selected to perpetuate the process. From their ranks would come the instructors at the service schools, the General Staff officers who coordinated army peacetime activities, and the planners of wartime mobilization and operations. Although the mission assigned the Staff College was difficult, the students enjoyed the year there more than the year of intense competition at the School of the Line. For one thing, after 1907

Staff College students had no examinations or grades. Further, students were at the Staff College because they were the best in the army.

In the decade before World War I, military art instruction at both the Leavenworth schools became increasingly sophisticated. As the quality of garrison school instruction improved, elementary subjects at the School of the Line were replaced with more difficult ones. Improvements at the school allowed the Staff College to drop some subjects and add others. Independent study, with increasing emphasis on research in military history, was the trend at the Staff College. As instructors became familiar with the tactical and doctrinal issues of that era, the schools began using more textbooks and problem-solving works prepared at Leavenworth rather than by foreigners. Nonetheless the foreign influence at the schools remained important.

In all armies tactics underwent reexaminations in the early 1900s. The Boer War, the Russo-Japanese War, and technical developments in weaponry forced military thinkers to reconsider previously accepted doctrine. As in other areas, many armies followed the tactics of the Germans. Not all armies blindly accepted the German example but nearly all studied the Germans and made allowances for differences in national circumstances.

Within the German Army, three distinct tactical schools existed. The radical innovators claimed that the Boer War had proved existing methods were wrong. Based on how they thought the British should have attacked the Boers, the radicals advocated an extreme open order of attack with subordinate leaders having wide latitude in carrying out their mission. The conservatives wanted to maintain cohesion of the attacking troops and retain close control by all commanders. Between their two views were the moderates, interested in a well-reasoned balance. German tactics tended toward the conservative although existing German regulations allowed sufficient latitude to subordinate commanders and stressed the offensive.[6]

The United States Army adopted much of German tactical doctrine and instruction techniques. A 1907 lecturer at Leavenworth declared: "Even the United States, whose military policy and institutions possess so little in common with those of the

German Empire, have not failed to follow in the wake of our European contemporaries. Our Field Service Regulations unmistakeably show the impress of German thought. Von Moltke teaches us our strategy, Griepenkerl writes our orders, while Von der Goltz tells us how they should be executed."[7]

Some American officers criticized what they considered an overreliance on foreign methodology and doctrine. In an extreme case, during World War I Robert L. Bullard, soon to be the Second Army commander, admonished two Leavenworth graduates in his command for being so "impressed with the efficiency of the Germans as soldiers that they have plainly weakened their own courage in the face of the Germans."[8] Leavenworth officials were usually less critical. They acknowledged the debt owed the Europeans but believed the eclecticism of American military education and doctrine was an advantage.[9]

Major John F. Morrison, for six years the dominant personality at Leavenworth, reported to the schools in September 1906 as an assistant instructor in military art, took over the department one year later, and remained there until 1912, eventually as assistant commandant and acting commandant. An 1881 graduate of West Point, Morrison had been a student in the second class at the School of Application for Infantry and Cavalry (1885) and had taught at Leavenworth for one year just before the Spanish-American War. More importantly for his development as an educator, for three years he had been the professor of military science and tactics at Kansas State Agricultural College, where he had taught a regular college course in physics, studied chemistry, and did considerable reading in military history and minor tactics. His work with the corps of cadets earned praise from the president of the university and from War Department inspectors. The president credited Morrison with stimulating interest among the students in the military department, which was in marked contrast to the situation under his predecessor. At an early period in his career Morrison already demonstrated his ability as an instructor, particularly of tactics.[10]

His understanding of troops and tactics further developed during periods of field service on the frontier in the 1880s, in Cuba in 1898 (for which he subsequently received a Silver Star "for

gallantry in action against Spanish forces at El Caney"), and in
the Philippines from 1899 to 1904. As a military attaché with
the Japanese (March-November 1904), Morrison was able to
study the education, training, organization, tactics, and operations of a first-class army and witness the biggest battle since
Sedan. The experience was so enlightening that Morrison, then
a captain, claimed he would not have traded it for a two-step
promotion to lieutenant colonel.[11]

The Manchurian experience had reinforced Morrison's tactical
ideas. Although Japanese infantry tactics offered "nothing
startling new," Morrison noted that they had not adopted an
extreme extended order in attack formations as some tacticians
advocated as a result of the Boer War. Morrison believed the
most significant Japanese tactical error was to assault along the
entire line rather than attempt to breach the Russian front and
then concentrate forces to exploit the breach. Finally Manchuria convinced Morrison that infantry frontal attacks could carry
strongly entrenched positions if the troops were well trained
and well led and if the commander was willing to accept casualties: "The right kind of infantry can carry anything if you
have enough of it. It is cheaper to do it some other way than
by frontal attack if possible but frontal attacks can win. . . . It
isn't the Arty. [artillery] that does the killing it is the little
steel jacketed rifle bullet."[12]

After returning from the Russo-Japanese War, Morrison attended the Army War College for one year where Bell recruited
him for the military art department at Leavenworth. Morrison's
experience in Manchuria greatly influenced Bell to select him
as an assistant instructor with the intention that he would soon
take over the department.[13]

Leaving Leavenworth in 1912, Morrison held a succession
of commands—a battalion at Vancouver Barracks, a regiment
on the Mexican border, all American troops at Tientsin, China,
and finally, during 1917, training camps in the southern United
States. For three months in 1917 he went to France to observe
Allied tactics, training, and organization. Briefly (January-March
1918) he put this and his previous experience to good use as
director of training for the entire army. Unfortunately his knowl-

edge was wasted as he subsequently commanded a single training division for three months and spent the remaining four
years of his career in largely administrative roles commanding
the Western Department, then the Southeastern Department,
and the IV Corps Area. He retired in December 1921.

The Morrison years at Leavenworth (1906-12) were fruitful,
exciting, and important. Morrison implemented significant
changes in the curriculum, instruction methods, and objectives
of the military art department. Although the schools had already
accepted the applicatory method of instruction, Morrison reinforced and refined the system. Throughout the army he had
the reputation as a good teacher, tactician, and officer.

The greatest praise came from his students, who years later
would proudly proclaim: "I was a Morrison man." They considered him the "master-mind" of the pre-World War I army,
the "No. 1 tactician of the Army," and "a real authority on
modern methods of war."[14] The students liked Morrison for
his personality, teaching ability, and straightforward, common-
sense manner. He could be rough on those who neglected
fundamental tactical principles, and he seldom complimented
students for good work. George C. Marshall remembered that
each problem Morrison designed "contained a knockout if
you failed to recognize the principle involved in meeting the
situation." Perhaps Marshall exaggerated when he proclaimed:
"He taught me all I had ever known of tactics."[15] But surely
Morrison taught Marshall and the others a great deal. These
"Morrison men" were anxious to spread the doctrine they
had learned and in the process credited their teacher with bringing about great and important changes in the army. For his
part, Morrison was self-effacing in his praise of the "progressive
set of youngsters" who had become his disciples.[16]

To perpetuate his ideas, ensure uniformity of instruction,
and maintain stability in the military art curriculum, Morrison
recruited Staff College graduates as assistant instructors. Using
some recent graduates as instructors was General Bell's idea,
but Morrison continued this practice after Bell went to Washington. The most outstanding of the assistant instructors were
Morrison men—Marshall, Arthur L. Conger, Stuart Heintzel-

man, Harold B. Fiske, Hugh A. Drum, LeRoy Eltinge, and
James W. McAndrew, to name a few. A number of these assistant
instructors, with the encouragement of Morrison, translated
foreign tactical works, wrote original books on American tactics,
and prepared problem-solving studies.[17]

The most ambitious of these projects was the 1908 publication of seventeen problems, contributed by Morrison and eight
military art instructors, *Studies in Minor Tactics*. Each problem
described a tactical situation (for example, attack over open
ground by infantry, forcing a defile, attack on a convoy) and
outlined one solution to the problem presented. The discussion
included much exposition on why a particular course was followed and the possible consequences of alternative solutions.
This 1908 publication had a lofty goal: "In most of the studies
an endeavor has been made to set forth certain principles of
minor tactics, but also to enable the reader to form for himself a mental picture of the manner in which troops might well
be handled in case the conditions assumed in the various studies
actually existed in the field."[18] Although the School of the
Line eventually discontinued using *Studies in Minor Tactics*,
the tactical books that replaced it had much the same format
and purpose. Morrison was the intellectual godfather of *Studies*
and thus the progenitor of other American problem-solving
books that followed.

As head of the military art department, from 1907 to 1909
Morrison rearranged the School of the Line curriculum, consoli-
dating some courses and adding more material to others. The
principal means of instruction continued to be the applicatory
method, with each part of the course including numerous practical problems.

Part I, or minor tactics, included problems involving forces
of a single arm from a squad to battalion. In part II the problems
involved units of two arms not exceeding the size of a regiment.
The class read, studied, and discussed Otto F. Griepenkerl's
Letters on Applied Tactics for part III. Because this was a comprehensive discussion of troop leading in twenty-five separate
tactical situations, Griepenkerl's became the most important,
widely used book in the Leavenworth curriculum. A general

review of tactics, including map problems and terrain exercises, made up the work in part IV. During 1907-08 Morrison expanded the work in war games from six to fifteen because he thought the games were "one of the best methods of teaching or acquiring a practical knowledge of tactics," and students found them "very valuable."[19]

In 1909 Morrison added a fifth part to tactics—study and solution of divisional tactical and strategical problems. The text, personally selected by Morrison, was Albert Buddecke's *Tactical Decisions and Orders:* "A study in troop leading (based on the operations of an independent division) for individual instruction." This problem-solving work analyzed the operations of an infantry division, with a cavalry brigade attached, over an eight-day period. In addition to Buddecke, the Line class solved ten other divisional problems. Previously systematic study of division-sized units had not been undertaken at the school. After inclusion of Buddecke, however, the school geared its course to units the size of a division, while the Staff College concentrated on larger forces.[20]

By 1912 the tactical work at the School of the Line had reached a standard that satisfied even Morrison, then assistant commandant. He called it "a decided improvement," "much more satisfactory." The faculty had doubled the amount of work in troop leading and transferred work previously offered at the Staff College to the School of the Line. Morrison explained: "The work that belonged in the Line Class year has been taken from the Staff Class and placed in the former and the Staff Class now is almost entirely devoted to preparation for the higher staff duties." Tactical study and troop leading was now nearly the exclusive province of the School of the Line.[21]

During the years from 1913 to 1916, the tactical curriculum remained relatively stable. The five-part course in tactics, begun under Morrison, continued, as did the applicatory method. Griepenkerl, Buddecke, von Alten, von der Goltz, and the American-authored problem-solving books remained. Morrison's influence was apparent in the arrangement of the curriculum, the applicatory method, and the books used. There was more to the curriculum than methodology, however, and Morrison's ideas on tactics shaped the course content as well.

As had Wagner, Swift, and other tactical instructors who had preceded him at Leavenworth, Morrison believed that tacticians were made "by practice in applying the fundamental principles of tactics to concrete cases; by the drilling of the mind to work in the right channel, to think of all conditions that surround the problem and to do it quickly; and above all, by bringing good common sense to bear." Practical problems were important because in Morrison's opinion there was little difference between exercises and war except "great physical danger and more or less excitement."[22] Practice in problem solving was more important than learning principles. Flexibility, adaptability, and common sense were the guidewords. Yet Morrison's tactical instruction included a number of common, often interrelated, themes, which were usually verbalized in his lectures and hidden in the practical problems he prepared for the students.

Whether on the defensive or in an offensive, Morrison emphasized officers should make simple plans but execute them vigorously. Complicated plans would assuredly fail in the confusion, friction, and fog of war. Once committed to an attack a commander could only push it forward, halt it, or retreat. There was little room for maneuver in combat on the modern battlefield. The judicious employment of reserves was nearly the only means at a commander's disposal to influence a battle already underway. Timely and vigorous commitment of reserves, however, was crucial. Wise use of resources, particularly manpower, was an essential decision for a tactician, the more so when engaging reserves: "Do not send them in in driblets."[23]

Because the offensive was basically a stronger means of combat, Morrison devoted more thought and analysis to it, although he admitted that locally the defensive often held advantages. The greatest offensive advantage was in its choice of a line of action. The initiative that attacking troops held in determining where, when, and how combat would commence could yield material benefits, but activity provided psychological advantages as well. Men on the attack could endure more than those standing on the defense. Dead and wounded comrades were left behind a vigorous, rapid advance so the sights and sounds of suffering would not affect the nerves of attackers as they might defenders. Morrison was very much attuned to the vagaries of the human element in warfare and the psychological impact of fire superiority. Leadership, he contended, could make the difference between one unit breaking under fire after suffering 6 percent casualties while another unit stood fast with 30 percent loss.[24]

Morrison prescribed no normal attack formations or methods because "any particular case is influenced by innumerable circumstances varying with each case." The terrain, objectives, arms, enemy, and even political conditions affected formations and methods. In a frontal assault, fire action, depth of formation, and advance by rushes were the essential means to reach the enemy positions. Morrison continued to reiterate that frontal attacks must be made and could succeed. Commanders should avoid them if possible, particularly on a broad front, but at some point nearly every attack became frontal. Once commenced, a frontal attack had to be pressed strongly. Attaining and maintaining fire superiority was crucial to subdue enemy fire, reduce casualties, and permit attacking forces to reach their objectives. Attackers would advance by rushes, taking advantage of cover and the supporting fire. While one portion of the line advanced, the remainder fired on the enemy. Thin lines of reinforcements would be pushed forward successively into the firing line and on joining would ideally carry that line forward in their advance. Finally, Morrison preached that for the final assault on enemy positions, if previous steps had been correctly followed, the attackers would be aligned in formations in depth. Constantly feeding the firing line would ensure sufficient troops for the final assault, for consolidation of the objective, and for pursuit of a defeated enemy.[25]

Essentially the tactical principles Morrison taught conformed to the *Field Service Regulations*, which after 1905 was the authority on which all tactical instruction at Leavenworth was based, as well as the basis for the organization, operations, and tactics of troops in the field. There were a few differences, how-

ever, between what Leavenworth and Morrison taught and what
the *Regulations* proclaimed as American doctrine. For instance,
the 1910 edition defined a field army as a command composed
of two or more divisions; Leavenworth continued to use the
more German designation of *army corps*. Similarly the 1910
Regulations, largely at the instance of General Bell, advocated
the use of bayonets in the final stages of an assault.[26] Based on
his experience in Manchuria, Morrison believed bayonets were
but a minor factor in modern warfare.[27] Morrison's use of tactical lessons from the war in Manchuria was a good example of
how recent military history furnished material for study and
analysis at the School of the Line.

Military history was always an important part of the Leavenworth curriculum, but especially at the Staff College where for
several years it consumed nearly half the instruction time in
military art. Leavenworth instructors were aware that the study
of past battles could easily become a useless pedantic exercise.
But if history showed why armies won or lost battles, it could
lead to greater understanding of tactics and strategy. Campaigns
of the American Civil War received the most attention, but
other American wars, European conflicts, the South African
War, and the Russo-Japanese War were also studied. At the
School of the Line instruction was by lecture and textbook
readings. History at the Staff College also included lectures
and discussions but increasingly came to rely on learning by
doing. Eventually it included a sophisticated course in historical
research.

From 1904 through 1916 military history instruction at
Leavenworth was principally in the hands of three officers: Matthew F. Steele, Arthur L. Conger, and Stuart Heintzelman.
Steele and Conger represented two phases in the evolution of
the military history curriculum and had rather different views
on how the course should be taught; Heintzelman followed Conger's lead. Steele lectured on past campaigns, illustrating enduring military principles. On the other hand, Conger was less certain that the passive exchange of knowledge by lectures would
have a lasting impact, regardless of how enduring the principles.
By immersion in the details of a particular campaign, through

means of original research in primary documents, Conger thought an officer's power of judgment, analytical ability, and appreciation for the wide variety of tactical possibilities could be improved. For Steele the lessons of history were important; for Conger the process by which students deduced the lessons for themselves was more important.

Steele graduated from West Point in 1883 and served mostly in command billets until his assignment to Leavenworth in 1903. His professional attainments were good but not outstanding, although he did enjoy writing. On two occasions, once for criticizing the sentence of a court-martial and once for an article critical of the army's policy toward black troops, his writing prompted reprimands from the War Department.[28] Within the limitations of the lecture format, Steele was a good Leavenworth instructor. During his five years at the schools he continually revised the lectures and eventually published them as *American Campaigns.*

Steele's work was not particularly original and espoused no firm theory or doctrine. He used history to instruct and to illustrate the theories of others. Although *American Campaigns* remained a military textbook at West Point until World War II, Steele formulated no clear strategic deductions. For instance, he never made clear whether the objective of strategy should be a city, the enemy's army, or some political goal. Indeed Steele variously stated that Richmond, or the Army of Northern Virginia, or the morale of the southern people was the objective of the Union Army. His obvious contradictions emphasized the absence of a distinctive American strategical doctrine during these years.[29]

If *American Campaigns* was not especially useful or clear on strategy, it nonetheless filled a need because there was no similar survey of American wars. At the tactical, operational level, Steele did illustrate useful lessons. In discussing General Pope's conduct during the Second Battle of Bull Run, he emphasized the necessity of timely information on which to base an estimate of the situation. Because Pope had no clear plan of operation and received contradictory information, he changed his mind with each new report and issued new orders. The resulting

marching and countermarching "wore his men out" and destroyed
their confidence in him. The battle was lost because Pope "never
had a true conception of the situation."[30] Because Leavenworth
education made much of a correct estimate of the situation followed by timely issuance of orders, such examples were useful
object lessons.

When Arthur L. Conger succeeded Steele as military history
instructor, the principle means of instruction changed. Albert
Buddecke, a German tactical authority of the period, pointed
out that military history was useful only if the student could
grasp and synthesize the real conditions and enter into the
thoughts of the leading personalities: "The education of the
tactician demands . . . a productive activity, in the exercise of
which he is confronted by questions still unsolved, which he
himself must solve."[31] Conger, who had translated Buddecke,
tried through original historical research to engage Staff College students in a "productive activity."

Conger graduated from Harvard in 1894, where he had studied
classical languages, Eastern religions, and music. He received a
Regular Army commission as a result of volunteer service during
the Spanish-American War. He was a Morrison man, recruited
from the Staff class to become an assistant instructor upon
Steele's relief from the schools. Unlike Steele he was not a good
lecturer; indeed one student declared that during Conger's lectures: "Everybody goes to sleep."[32] Conger had considerable
graduate training in historical research and writing, at Harvard,
Nebraska, Heidelberg, and, finally, Berlin, where one of his instructors was the noted military historian Hans Delbrück. He
taught at Leavenworth on two separate occasions, 1907-10 and
1913-16, longer than any other instructor. During the war he
served primarily in the intelligence section at Pershing's headquarters but also led a brigade at the height of the Meuse-Argonne fighting in October 1918. Immediately after the armistice
Conger conducted delicate negotiations with leading German
military leaders and eventually became the American military
attaché in Berlin.[33]

As an instructor at Leavenworth and in his subsequent intelligence work, Conger was a good synthesizer, able to distinguish the crucial from the unimportant. He had a quick, facile mind. His Harvard mentor, R. M. Johnston, considered Conger a "first-rate" historian. A student and eventually fellow staff officer in France, John M. Palmer, regarded him as a "brilliant and sometimes eccentric genius."[34] Although not a good speaker, Conger proved an admirable instructor. Through his insight and a graduate seminar format, he was able to involve the students in the interworkings of military campaigns. With his guidance they worked out the details of tactical and stragical movements and drew their own conclusions as to lessons to be learned.

During 1907 and 1908 Conger first lectured at the Staff College on the techniques of historical research and required students to prepare original research papers. This first year he limited research to a single topic, the Peninsula campaign of 1862. On a large-scale map of the region students followed the day-to-day movements of both armies. By weighing evidence from many sources, they ascertained what happened and why.[35] Considering all aspects of a campaign, analyzing data, and preparing studies was valuable training for potential General Staff officers and was similar to the work many Leavenworth graduates did on the staff of the American Expeditionary Forces.

During the next few years, Conger and his successor, Captain Stuart Heintzelman, expanded this work. Whereas in the first year the students researched the Peninsula, the next year the college doubled the time for historical research, which permitted study of seven campaigns: Fort Donelson, the Peninsula, Grant's move to south of the James, Austerlitz, Waterloo, Metz, and Paardeberg. The Army Service School Library acquired several copies of the massive War Department documentary compendium, *The War of the Rebellion: A Compilation of the Official Records of the Union and Confederate Armies*, to facilitate research in primary sources. Because of easy access to the official records, most research was on Civil War campaigns. The library also acquired numerous secondary sources and memoirs to allow work on foreign campaigns. Conger and the department of languages further facilitated primary research by translating documents related to the battle of St. Privat and Napoleon's 1800 campaign.[36]

The methods of historical research at the college were not superficial and were worthy of professional historians. Professor Fred Morrow Fling, of the University of Nebraska, assisted Conger and Heintzelman in preparing the course. Twice, for short periods, Fling taught at the college. In January 1914 he wrote of a Staff College historical exercise he had recently witnessed:

> The topic for investigation was the capture of Yorktown. Each member of the class was provided with copies of the *Records of Rebellion.* The work assigned the class for a written report had been (1) to date the documents— determining the hour when they were issued for the purpose of determining the order of events; (2) to establish the facts; (3) to make a connected statement concerning the course of the engagement; and (4) to comment upon the operation from the point of view of military science. . . . The class exercise was intensely interesting. It was a genuine graduate seminar in which the best kind of critical training was being given and the most satisfactory results obtained.[37]

Although the methods of historical research at the college were similar to those followed in graduate school history departments, the goal of the Staff College was to improve the professional ability of its students. Conger thought that studying military history was one way for officers to form a "clear mental conception of war."[38] It taught them the relative value of primary and secondary sources and how to distinguish between credible and dubious statements and between sound and false deductions. This method of instruction fostered critical thinking applicable not only to historical evidence but to experience in war: "For the same tests of 'good faith' and 'accuracy' and the determination of 'weight' which we learn to employ in dealing critically with historic sources must be applied surely, quickly and instinctively to all the bits of information which come to us through the fog of war, if we are to read the situation aright and not be led into wrong measures."[39]

Leavenworth did not use military history to justify the latest tactical or strategical doctrine.[40] History was a means of instruction that allowed students to arrive at their own deductions regarding proper doctrine and was a sufficiently rigid analytical tool to ensure some consensus on what was proper. More importantly military history provided an unlimited number of situations that students could analyze from the tactical, strategical, logistical, or technological standpoint. As participants, albeit secondhand, in actual situations, they had an opportunity to apply principles previously learned and test their tactical and judgment skills.

At the School of the Line tactical and leadership considerations dominated the solutions of problems. The Staff College course approached problems "from the point of view of the staff officer; to try to give the class an idea of the problems that must in war confront the man who is acting as Chief of Staff for a division or a larger unit."[41] In addition to the changed emphasis in the practical problems, instruction at the college included a course on the duties of the general staff, begun in 1907 by Morrison. Perhaps more than other military art courses, the duties of the general staff involved a simple exchange of information made necessary by the almost total ignorance of American officers about such a staff. In particular the college dealt with the operational responsibilities of staff officers in the field. But the techniques were much the same for the War Department General Staff where Staff College graduates fully expected to serve.

Fritz Bronsart von Schellendorff's *Duties of the General Staff* was the basis for the staff course. It was not used as a text but more as a reference work, supplemented by lectures, other literature, and lengthy class discussions. This book, which contained information on the history, theory, organization, and operation of general staffs, with the Prussian General Staff as a model, remained the most important source on staff duties used at the college.

Most of the book discussed activities of general staff officers

in active campaigns. According to von Schellendorff, they had
eight tasks to perform during battle. Not every staff officer was
concerned with each, but the staff as an entity was responsible
for reconnoitering the enemy and the terrain in the vicinity of
operations, reporting the progress of battle to the commander,
keeping track of enemy and friendly positions, conveying orders
to subordinate commanders, assisting the subordinates in changing their dispositions, selecting positions for artillery, explaining matters to subordinates needing information and assistance,
and looking after casualties and prisoners. Basically general staff
officers gathered information, assisted the commander in preparing a plan of action, translated the plan into orders, and ensured that subordinates carried out the orders. In each of these
tasks, they relieved the commander of much detail. They were
the men in the middle, not commanding directly but sometimes
issuing orders in the name of the commander. Von Schellendorff dwelt at length on the personal equation of general staff
duty, especially the relationship between staff officers and commanders.[42] As this was the most difficult yet the most important aspect of staff work, instructors at the Staff College also
contemplated the problem.

Major James W. McAndrew, an instructor at Leavenworth
and later Pershing's chief of staff, thought chiefs of staff of
tactical units should have considerable leeway in performing
their duties. In an article based on discussions at the Staff College, he wrote: "Is a chief of staff justified in modifying or al-
tering the orders of his superiors where he feels such orders are
faulty? We are treading on dangerous ground if we give either
an unqualified positive or negative answer to this question."
The idea that in some circumstances a chief of staff should alter or change orders, or initiate operations in the name of his
superior, undoubtedly appalled old Army officers. It caused
misunderstanding and friction in France in 1918 when Leavenworth-trained division, corps, and army staff officers served
commanders, most of whom had no formal staff education.
As had von Schellendorff, McAndrew stressed that chiefs of
staff should not seek to usurp the authority of the commander
but should attempt to remain at his side whenever possible.

On occasions that require separation from the commander, chiefs of staff should not hesitate to act on their own initiative. When a chief of staff should act depended on his self-confidence and professional knowledge.[43] Prior instruction could not alter the personal equation other than to delineate potential problem areas, but staff officers thoroughly versed in the responsibilities and authority of their position and with solid backgrounds in tactics, strategy, and logistics would likely accomplish their duties.

Besides the necessary information on the functions of a general staff, the potential staff officers at the college were given some opportunity to apply their newly acquired knowledge. After the creation of the War Department General Staff in 1903, the army began preparing contingency war plans. Although Staff College students did not make formal war plans, they prepared mobilization or concentration plans that involved the movement of large bodies of troops great distances and could become integral parts of the basic plans. The details of one such plan, prepared as a map problem by the 1910-11 Staff class, was fifteen single-spaced typed pages. In this problem the students planned a move of thirteen divisions, located at posts throughout the United States, to Seattle and San Francisco as quickly as possible. The solution included the order in which the troops would move, the number of trains required to move each division and its supplies, expedients to use in obtaining the needed trains, the routes and schedules for the trains, the places of debarkation, and the complete account of supplies each division needed. The class had two days in which to complete the work.[44]

The complicated, meticulous calculation required in concentration plans was the most difficult work at either school. As such it was a fitting culmination to the military art curriculum. Additionally because the General Staff used the concentrations plans prepared at the college, the work helped bridge the gap between Leavenworth as an intellectual center and the real needs of the army.

From 1904 to 1916 the amount of instruction time at the school and the college for military art increased at the expense of the other departments—military engineering, law, languages, and care of troops. Although knowledge of the subjects covered in military art was essential for the intellectual development of a professional officer, the material covered in the other courses was also useful. Moreover the work in the other departments complemented the military art course.

Instruction in the department of care of troops considered sanitation problems of units in the field. It aptly supplemented the practical, tactical problems that dominated the military art curriculum and was a clear reaction to the sanitation debacles that had characterized American operations in 1898. Although elementary and not entirely successful, language instruction was supposed to prepare some officers for duty in the Spanish-speaking insular possessions and introduce others to French and German so they could deal with the European professional literature. Experience in civil disturbances during the late nineteenth century and in governing civilian populations in overseas possessions, as well as more routine use by officers of military and international law, necessitated some legal instruction. The law curriculum was general, geared to legal problems that line officers, not judge advocates, would encounter. Courses in law and languages were not always successful. School of the Line students particularly disliked Spanish and in only a year learned little of lasting value. Yet instruction techniques were modern, including moot courts in law and use of phonograph records in languages, which indicated some appreciation for pedagogical advances in civilian universities.[45]

About half of the instruction in military engineering, the second most important department, dealt with surveying, map reading, and topographical sketching; Captain Edwin T. Cole, the senior engineering instructor, called this work the "key to the study of Military Art." Nearly all tactical problems, whether in training or actual combat, were solved on contour maps. As Cole put it: "There is but one way to become a first-class map reader, and that is by first becoming a map maker."[46] Among the specific skills taught in the topography courses were how to estimate distances; how terrain features mask prospective routes of advance from enemy observation and fire and how to recognize these terrain features on a map; and how best to use the ground from a military point of view. Above all the students learned to appreciate and understand the relation between maps and the ground forms that maps represented.

Field fortifications was the second half of the engineering curriculum. Lectures on the use of field fortifications in the Civil War and the Russo-Japanese War usually gave the course a historical perspective, although most of the work was practical. For instance students selected sites for fortifications to protect a critical position, such as a bridge, and prescribed the type of position needed. Apart from the technical questions of how to build field fortifications and where to locate them, Leavenworth tried to cultivate an appreciation for when and why to use them. Although American tactics in the years before World War I emphasized that only offensive action could produce decisive results, the proper use of fortifications could protect friendly forces, diminish the effect of hostile fire, and limit the enemy's ability to maneuver. One Leavenworth text declared: "Too early, too extensive, and too frequent use of field fortifications are certain to injure the offensive spirit of leaders and troops, sacrifice the maneuver power and surrender tactical advantage to the adversary. On the other hand, a total neglect of the benefit to be derived from the employment of field fortifications will involve needless and heavy losses, and, against a skillful adversary, will lead to disaster."[47] The school tried to teach students the essential point: to decide when field fortifications were necessary and when they hindered offensive action. In World War I the past study of fortifications clearly did not hamper American offensive spirit.

A failure to appreciate the full impact of technology on warfare was the greatest shortcoming of the Leavenworth curriculum. With the exception of an occasional student research paper, almost no attention was given to aeronautics at either the School of the Line or Staff College. Although by 1916 automobiles, motor trucks, and tractors had become common means of conveyance, the horse remained the principal source of locomotion so far as Leavenworth was concerned.

Perhaps more surprisingly, instruction on field artillery and machine guns, the two weapons that did most of the killing in World War I, was inadequate. Until the war in Europe demonstrated their effectiveness, instructors continued to underestimate grossly the number of machine guns adequate for supporting infantry.[48] Artillery instruction was largely by means of lectures and demonstrations, although solutions of some tactical problems required students to deploy field artillery. After 1910 artillery demonstrations became rare because the War Department transferred field artillery units from Fort Leavenworth. The result was lamentable; as one artillery instructor explained: "It is manifestly almost useless to try to teach a student theoretically the use of an instrument he has never seen."[49] Many of the lectures on field artillery dealt with technical matters that provided no useful insight into the powers and limitations of the arm and its tactical use. In particular cooperation between artillery and the other arms was not explained fully. Frequent errors in the use of field artillery on map problems at the school was one result.[50] Although the American army learned quickly, it went into World War I with an inadequate conception of the place of field artillery. Leavenworth mirrored this shortcoming.

Because the course largely ignored these important, technologically advanced weapons and transportation systems, Leavenworth contributed little to the technological revolution in warfare. Yet in the operational realm—management of armies in the field—it was innovative. It stimulated the study of tactical developments in foreign armies. The military art courses dealt with practical tactical situations involving units much larger than those previously studied at American military schools. Finally Leavenworth created a system and inculcated its students in that system. Where previously commanders and subordinates had extemporized such essentials as issuing operational orders, Leavenworth established a pattern to which all future commanders and their subordinates were expected to adhere. The course would not supply all the answers. After exposure to the most current military thought and immersion in the system by means of extensive practical work, however, it was expected that graduates possessed the necessary analytical tools to solve military problems.

Most of the Leavenworth curriculum was not difficult. What made the course hard, especially at the School of the Line, was the student competition for the Staff class and a very heavy work load consisting of repetitive practical problems that required considerable study outside the classroom. The military art courses at the School of the Line were very taxing of the ability and endurance of students and instructors alike. Graduates remembered doing "problem after problem" and of having "little change in the monotony."[51] But with constant practice they became proficient tacticians able to solve problems under stress.

The stress created by the Leavenworth course was principally mental. During each spring, however, when both the engineering and military art curriculum required much outdoor work, it was not unusual for students to spend most of every day riding horseback or walking. The schedule during May and June of 1909 was typical: May 29 (Saturday), war games in the forenoon; May 31, "Rode out Atchinson Pike and solved a fortification problem. Returned at 5 P.M."; "June 1, Staff ride with Captain Hanna in charge, rode all day"; June 2, rode out Atchinson Pike again for fortification problem in morning, engineering demonstration of pontoons on Merritt Lake in afternoon; June 3, problem in examination of bridges; June 7-10: "Terrain exercises all day."[52] Many Leavenworth men would have agreed with George C. Marshall when he claimed: "It was the hardest work I ever did in my life."[53]

While work at Leavenworth did not make finished and polished professional soldiers, the course had put officers "on the path and pointed out the direction [they] should travel" to accomplish that.[54] The experience at the schools improved the self-confidence of many officers, even those not making the Staff class, and motivated them to continue professional study. The easygoing anti-intellectual atmosphere of the Old Army made serious independent study difficult without a rigorous framework such as Leavenworth afforded. Marshall first began reading the professional literature at the schools. He also developed good work habits and a thoroughness that were beneficial later in his career:

> While . . . I learned little I could use . . . I learned how
> to learn. . . . I began to develop along more stable lines.
> Leavenworth was immensely instructive, not so much be-
> cause the course was perfect—because it was not—but the
> associations with the officers, the reading we did and the
> discussion and the leadership . . . of a man like Morrison
> had a tremendous effect, certainly on me, and I think on
> most of my class.[55]

As Marshall suggested, associations developed among officers at Leavenworth had an important impact on the future course of individual careers and, in some cases, on the development of the entire army. The motivated, career-oriented, select group of professionals at Leavenworth made associations formed at the schools particularly important and usually long lasting. Contacts made at the schools had more than just social value. Numerous graduates attributed later success, at least in part, to associations first formed at Leavenworth.[56] Unlike administrative duties at a garrison or commanding a seventy-five man company, Leavenworth gave officers an opportunity to demonstrate intellectual and leadership ability. Colleagues remembered these traits later. Another of Marshall's classmates believed that at Leavenworth Marshall began to be a "marked man" impressing people as being "so darned efficient."[57]

Although Marshall was by no means typical, either as a student or later in his career, the people he met at Leavenworth, the friendships he formed there, and the way these affected his career were representative of other students' experience. His class at the School of the Line (1907) included eight future generals. Classmates, instructors, pupils (from the two years he taught at the school), and other officers assigned to the post included numerous men who later served in important general staff and command billets in the AEF. As an operations officer at several levels in the AEF, Marshall dealt daily with many of these same men. The associations and common experience they had at Leavenworth facilitated these later, more critical contacts.[58]

Because Leavenworth taught a systematic solution of operational problems, the personal contacts at the schools were particularly important. For the system to succeed officers had to be assured that their peers understood how the system functioned. Officers left the schools knowing that other Leavenworth graduates "spoke the same language." Besides the common techniques of problem solving and order writing they learned there, the shared experience of competition for the Staff class, the constant grind of repetitious map problems, and the social contacts contributed to the socialization of Leavenworth men. As a group they developed a professional self-awareness, an image of army officers as true professionals. At Leavenworth a significant amount of professional knowledge was passed on, especially in the tactics, general staff, and military engineering courses. The curriculum also helped officers to recognize the intellectual, theoretical basis of their profession while concurrently offering an opportunity to practice some of the more difficult professional duties by means of the applicatory method. If the Leavenworth curriculum helped prepare officers for the professional challenges they would face, how they performed after graduation largely determined the schools' success and impact on the service.

NOTES

1. Alfred W. Bjornstad, "Tactical Instruction of Line Officers," *Infantry Journal* 7 (March 1911): 687.

2. LeRoy Eltinge, "Tactical Instruction of Officers," *Cavalry Journal* 20 (March 1910): 922-25.

3. Bjornstad, "Tactical Instruction," p. 708.

4. Colonel H. A. Greene 6th Ind. to Chief of Engineers to Adjutant General, November 29, 1915, file 6994; Greene to Adjutant General, January 30, 1915, file 537, Record Group 393, National Archives.

5. Brigadier General Eben Swift to Lieutenant Colonel James Mc-Andrew, May 12, 1917, file 537, RG 393.

6. Major de Pardieu, *A Critical Study of German Tactics*, trans.

Charles F. Martin (Fort Leavenworth: U. S. Cavalry Association, 1912).

7. Gilbert A. Youngberg, "The Present Tendencies of German Tactics," *Infantry Journal* 3 (January 1907): 30-55; Charles S. Lincoln, "The Development of Infantry Organization and Tactics," *Infantry Journal* 7 (January 1911): 586-600.

8. Colonel Robert L. Bullard, June 15, 1917, diary book no. 8, Robert L. Bullard Papers, Library of Congress.

9. Major Eben Swift to Major John F. Morrison, May 14, 1906, file 4037, RG 393. Swift was then in France "trying to learn from the Europeans."

10. Inspector General Reports, April 30, 1888, October 23-24, 1889, and Officer's Individual Reports, May 1, 1890, December 15, 1891, file 1953-ACP-1887, RG 94.

11. Morrison to Charles Boardman, May 2, July 15, September 16, 1904, box 2, Charles R. Boardman Papers, State Historical Society of Wisconsin; Military Information Division, *Reports of the Military Observers in Manchuria during the Russo-Japanese War, Part I* (Washington, D.C.: GPO, 1906), pp. 98-99.

12. *Report of the Military Observers*, pt. I, pp. 95, 97; Morrison to Boardman, September 16, 1904, box 2, Boardman Papers.

13. See the large series of letters exchanged between Bell and Morrison during 1905 and 1906, file 4037, RG 393.

14. Arthur L. Conger quoted in Aileen B. Shurlock, *Biographical Sketch of A. L. Conger* (Oakland, Calif., 1955), p. 16; Forrest C. Pogue interview with Charles D. Herron, May 28, 1958; Charles D. Herron to author, March 28, 1970.

15. Marshall quoted in Forrest C. Pogue, *George C. Marshall: Education of a General* (New York: Viking Press, 1963), p. 99.

16. Morrison to George Van Horn Moseley, January 15, 1916, and note put on letter by Moseley sometime after World War I, Scrapbook of Selected Papers, 1899-1942, George Van Horn Moseley Papers, Library of Congress.

17. Examples include Oliver L. Spaulding's translation of Hans von Kiesling's *Battle Orders*, Spaulding's own *Notes on Field Artillery*, and Henry E. Eames's *The Rifle in War*.

18. Department of Military Art, *Studies in Minor Tactics* (Fort Leavenworth: Army Service Schools Press, 1908), p. iii.

19. "Report of the Senior Instructor in Military Art, SOL" (Morrison), in "Annual Report of the Commandant," 1908, RG 94.

20. Ibid., in "Annual Report of the Commandant," 1909, RG 94.

21. "Report of the Assistant Commandant, Army Service Schools"

(Morrison), in "Annual Report of the Commandant," 1912, RG 94.

22. John F. Morrison, *Seventy Problems—Infantry Tactics* (Fort Leavenworth: U. S. Cavalry Association, 1914), pp. 1, 168.

23. Ibid., pp. 6, 9.

24. Ibid., pp. 169-170.

25. Ibid., pp. 167, 177, 183.

26. Edgar Frank Raines, Jr., "Major General J. Franklin Bell and Military Reform: The Chief of Staff Years, 1906-1910" (Ph.D. diss., University of Wisconsin, 1976), pp. 482-83; War Department, *Field Service Regulations* (Washington, D.C.: GPO, 1910), pp. 165-66.

27. Morrison, *Seventy Problems*, pp. 168-69.

28. See files 1201814 and 1751837 filed with 2308-ACP-1890, RG 94.

29. Jay Luvaas, "Military History: An Academic Historian's Point of View," in Russell F. Weigley, ed., *New Dimensions in Military History* (San Rafael, Calif.: Presidio Press, 1976), pp. 31-32.

30. Matthew F. Steele, *American Campaigns* (Washington, D.C.: Byron S. Adams, 1909), p. 256.

31. Albert Buddecke, *Tactical Decisions and Orders*, trans. Arthur L. Conger (Kansas City: Franklin Hudson Publishing Co., 1908), p. 16.

32. Ola W. Bell, diary, March 25, 1915, United States Military Academy Library.

33. Fritz Epstein, "Zwischen Compiegne und Versailles: Geheime amerikanische Militärdiplomatie in der Periode des Waffenstillstandes 1918/19: Die Rolle des Obersten Arthur L. Conger," *Vierteljahrshefte für Zeitgeschichte* 4 (October 1955): 412-55.

34. Robert M. Johnston to Leonard Wood, January 31, 1914, box 76, Leonard Wood Papers, Library of Congress; chapter notes, vol. 5, box 16, John McAuley Palmer Papers, Library of Congress.

35. "Report of the Senior Instructor in Military Art, SC" (Morrison), in "Annual Report of the Commandant," 1908, RG 94.

36. Ibid., in "Annual Report of the Commandant," 1909; ibid. (Major Willard A. Holbrook), in "Annual Report of the Commandant," 1914, RG 94.

37. Frederick Morrow Fling, "Review of *Donelson Campaign Sources*," *American Historical Review* 19 (January 1914): 373.

38. For the purpose and methodology of military history in the army at this time, see Conger's statement in American Historical Association, *Annual Report for the Year 1912* (Washington, D.C.: GPO, 1914), 1: 167-72; Brigadier General M. M. Macomb, "The Scientific Study of Military History: Opening Address in the Military History Course at the Army War College," February 15, 1916, U. S. Army Military History Research Collection, Carlisle Barracks, Pennsylvania.

39. Fling, "Review of *Donelson,*" pp. 372-73.

40. Conger statement in American Historical Association, *Annual Report,* pp. 164-69; Herbert Rosinski, *The German Army* (Washington, D.C.: Infantry Journal Press, 1944), pp. 83-84, 164-66.

The Prussian General Staff produced many fine historical monographs during this era. Particularly in the aftermath of the War of 1866, von Moltke generated a spirit of investigation and desire to learn the truth about war. Some of the monographs produced on the 1870-71 war and on the Boer War, however, lacked this total objectivity. They sought to protect officers' reputations, to disparage the tactics and military systems of potential enemies, and to justify German military doctrine and policy.

41. "Military Art Report," in Annual Reports," 1908. RG 94.

42. Fritz Bronsart von Schellendorff, *The Duties of the General* Staff, trans. H. A. Bethell, J. H. V. Crowe, and F. B. Maurice (London: His Majesty's Stationary Office, 1907), pp. 3-4, 300-01.

43. James W. McAndrew, "The Chief of Staff," *Infantry Journal* 9 (September-October 1912): 181-214. For a discussion of the breakdown of this concept in the AEF, see Edward M. Coffman, "The American Military Generation Gap in World War I: The Leavenworth Clique in the A.E.F.," in William E. Geffen, ed., *Command and Commanders in Modern Warfare: Proceedings of the Second Military History Symposium, U. S. Air Force Academy* (Washington, D. C.: GPO, 1969), pp. 35-43.

44. Map Problem, 2d series, nos. 2 and 3, Military Art Department, Staff College, 1910-11, file 5240, RG 393; also E. L. King and W. C. Babcock, "Movement of a Cavalry Division," *Cavalry Journal* 24 (May 1914): 947-55.

45. Timothy K. Nenninger, "The Fort Leavenworth Schools: Postgraduate Military Education and Professionalization in the U. S. Army, 1880-1920," (Ph.D. diss., University of Wisconsin, 1974), pp. 240-58.

46. "Report of the Senior Instructor in Military Engineering, SOL" (Cole), in "Annual Report of the Commandant," 1908, RG 94.

47. Army Field Engineer School, *Notes on Field Fortifications* (Fort Leavenworth: Army Service Schools Press, 1914), pp. 5-6, 9.

48. See for instance, Charles Crawford, "Weapons and Munitions of War," *Cavalry Journal* 17 (April 1907): 621, which estimated two guns for every 1000 infantry. In 1918 the AEF had about 250 machine guns and automatic rifles for each infantry regiment of about 4,000 men.

49. Captain Dwight Aultman to Adjutant General, September 13, 1910, file 5226, RG 393.

50. Major Harry G. Bishop to Commandant, February 12, 1914, file 7197, RG 393.

51. Forrest C. Pogue interview with George C. Marshall, April 4, 1957; Ola W. Bell, diary, March 10, 1915.

52. Richard H. McMaster, diary, May-June 1909, South Carolinia Library, University of South Carolina.

53. Pogue interview with Marshall, April 4, 1957.

54. Captain R. M. Brambila to Secretary, September 14, 1906, file 5341, RG 393.

55. Marshall quoted in Pogue, *Education of a General*, p. 101.

56. Louis M. Nuttman to author, December 16, 1971.

57. Pogue interview with Herron, May 28, 1958.

58. Pogue, *Education of a General*, pp. 94, 107.

7

THE SCHOOLS
AND THE ARMY

Several factors affected Leavenworth's impact on the army and
influenced the rest of the service's image of the schools. From
an early date, the people at Leavenworth tried to combat the
image of graduates as impractical soldiers only suited for
"school-boy" details, as some critics of Leavenworth education
derisively charged. General Bell firmly believed that the intensive tactical instruction at the School of the Line qualified graduates for responsible command positions and for duties as divisional staff officers. Staff College graduates were expected to
dominate the Army War College and the War Department General Staff in peacetime and fill most of the staff positions and
some of the command billets of the field army in wartime.[1]
According to another commandant, William P. Burnham, all
graduates were stamped as Leavenworth men, which meant "advanced and up-to-date knowledge of the profession of arms."[2]
For a variety of reasons the results were more mixed than these
optimistic pronouncements.

Because of what they considered their superior training, many,
if not most, Leavenworth students did not want to return to
troop duty, where they would have been immersed in the petty
administrative details of commanding a company, following graduation. During his first year as commandant, Bell found the Staff

class and a large portion of the Infantry and Cavalry class seeking detached details to avoid regimental duty. Bell and the General Staff wanted graduates with troops where they could apply their newly learned skills at the most basic tactical level and thus spread Leavenworth methods and doctrine among all regiments of the Army.[3] The skills and knowledge acquired at the schools, however, were more immediately applicable in various detached service details, particularly on duty as instructors and staff officers, though not necessarily on the War Department General Staff. After 1912 the situation changed; service school graduates were required under the Manchu law to serve with their regiments for two years before again becoming eligible for detached service. One officer who obviously did not relish troop duty wrote to a friend at Leavenworth, "After two years in a tent fighting various insect pests from Galveston to Vera Cruz and back again, was glad to complete my two years Manchu without the loss of a day and get away."[4] Although they were not the only officers seeking detached service, Leavenworth men were viewed as the most pernicious of the Manchus.

Immediately after graduation many Leavenworth officers went to militia instruction and maneuver camps as instructors and umpires. Leavenworth had prepared them well for such duty. At these camps the graduates planned and umpired the maneuvers and exercises, as well as assisted with the administrative details of housing, feeding, and transporting many troops. Graduates could observe on a large scale and with live troops the lessons studied at the schools. These summer camps were among the few occasions when large, division-sized units were brought together in the peacetime army of the 1900s. One graduate reported: "The course was of material benefit to me at the maneuvers in Virginia last fall where, as aide to the Commander of the Fourth Brigade, Second Division, I could see matters in their proper perspective; understand clearly what was attempted; coordinate the different arms of the service in their movements and assist intelligently in the transmission of orders and information."[5] When Bell asked commanders of the 1906 camps to report on the performance of Leavenworth men, their reaction was favorable. Most agreed it was valuable experience for the young officers and demonstrated the "splendid work done at Leavenworth." Bell received only one critical report, but even the critic admitted that umpires who were Leavenworth graduates were better than those who were not.[6] In successive years graduates were requested for the camps of instruction because, according to the chief of the Division of Militia Affairs: "Their presence at such camps will be of great value to the militia."[7]

How graduates performed after returning to their regiments was important for determining Leavenworth's reputation throughout the army. It was also important for the development of an officer's career. Being a Leavenworth graduate usually helped but in itself was insufficient to ensure choice assignments and fast promotions. General Pershing later wrote of a close associate in the American Expeditionary Forces: "General Drum's work in the Philippines, at the Leavenworth Schools and on the border had attracted my attention, and on my personal request he accompanied me to France."[8] The schools prepared these chosen officers, but each had to demonstrate his ability in practical ways. Most did well not simply because they went to the schools but because they were better prepared than were nongraduates.

Because they were better prepared and knew it, graduates wanted to apply lessons they had learned. Seniors and subordinates in their regiments often, but not always, were anxious to hear their views on military matters. As one graduate noted: "Whether or not they thought the opinions were good is another matter but the fact of their asking for the opinions proved to me that they regarded the course at the Infantry and Cavalry School of some value."[9] During the years before World War I, the people at Leavenworth believed graduates were carrying on work of great value and contributed to the army more than could be expected from their small number.

A few students, however, considered their Leavenworth education of little value immediately after graduation. Because he was commanding only a company on the border in 1916, Louis M. Nuttman thought: "At Leavenworth I was trained for higher command and that came only after the war broke out."[10]

Graduates and nongraduates alike thought Leavenworth education showed. The schools had taught the importance of proper organization, of teamwork, and of tactical training. Much as Bell had wanted, upon return to their regiments these officers attempted to apply newly learned concepts to their duties. After leaving the Staff College in 1910, John M. Palmer was a company commander at Fort Douglas and in 1911 a brigade staff officer with the Maneuver Division at San Antonio. Rather than conduct the usual infantry drill, Palmer held small-scale field problems, pitting one of his platoons against another. In the post school for officers and NCOs for which he was responsible, Palmer introduced map problems rather than rely on the usual recitation method of instruction. The commander of the brigade in which Palmer served in 1911 chose him as the principal brigade staff officer largely on the basis of Palmer's Staff College education. Palmer had considerable responsibility and discretion in organizing the brigade staff and in planning and supervising brigade tactical exercises. The brigade staff was unique in that it remained a small tactical and training headquarters while other brigades in the division had large staffs created to handle administrative problems, most of which never occurred. Palmer's commander handled most of the administrative details personally.[11] Largely because of Palmer's efforts, officers in the brigade, from the brigadier to the youngest second lieutenant, were given new insights on tactics, training, and organization.

Younger officers in particular appreciated what Leavenworth men were attempting but also recognized there were limits on what could be accomplished. One young lieutenant remembered how Hugh Drum planned extensive field maneuvers and other innovative tactical exercises when Drum was a training officer with the Second Division at Texas City in 1914. Drum, recently graduated from the schools, and Bell, then the division commander, tried to impart some Leavenworth doctrine and methods to the troops.[12] In 1916 Perry L. Miles trained his battalion for open warfare according to what he had learned at Fort Leavenworth but "oblivious of the lessons the combatants in Europe were learning in the trenches."[13] Leavenworth training was most noticeable in maneuvers. One graduate, Charles D. Herron, and a future general of the army, Omar Bradley, remembered that Leavenworth men were often the only effective officers in conducting maneuvers.[14]

A Leavenworth education was not a tactical panacea, however. Officers had to apply correctly lessons learned in the classroom to the practical situations that confronted them in the field. Another young officer serving on the border in 1915 remembered that his company commander, although a Leavenworth and War College graduate, taught his subordinates nothing he had learned at the schools.[15] In training, a failure to apply the lessons taught at Leavenworth perpetuated ignorance, which could lead to future targedy. In combat a similar failure often brought immediate tragedy.

A distinguished graduate of the School of the Line and a Staff College graduate should have been an officer of discretion and a sound tactician. But Captain Charles T. Boyd, commanding two troops of cavalry on the Pershing expedition in June 1916, was not discreet and did not use good tactics when he met a force of Mexican soldiers at Carrizal. Although greatly outnumbered, warned by the Mexican commander not to advance, and operating under ambiguous orders, Boyd decided to attack. Rather than advancing by fire and maneuver, he led his dismounted troopers in a frontal assault. The Mexicans captured twenty-four of the cavalrymen, wounded twelve, and killed nine, including Boyd.[16] Although Mexican casualties were higher, it was a futile action and indicated that professional training was meaningless unless properly applied and tempered by common sense.

Graduation from Leavenworth excused an officer from portions of promotion examinations and from some courses at the garrison schools, although graduates did participate in the schools, many as instructors. After returning to his field artillery regiment following relief from Leavenworth, Captain Richard H. McMaster used Leavenworth methods when he taught the advanced and elementary garrison school courses and ran the noncommissioned officers school. When John F. Morrison commanded the Sixth Infantry, that unit's garrison courses used the applicatory method and emphasized writing field orders, the Leavenworth way, to solve tactical problems.[17] Those who taught at the garrison schools had a unique opportunity to transmit Leavenworth knowledge, to influence the minds of young officers, and to try to change the minds of some of the "old moss backs." For many Leavenworth graduates the garrison school provided a good review of the elementary material covered at the School of the Line. At some garrison schools, however, the instruction was inadequate. Captain William D. Chitty wrote disparagingly of the school at Fort Meade, South Dakota: "Our distinguished post commander is making a grand bluff at teaching us . . . by means of what he calls a map problem. It is about as much a map problem as I am a suffragette."[18]

What Leavenworth graduates did shaped the attitudes of non-Leavenworth men toward the school. As in most human endeavors attitudes were based on perceptions, sometimes irrationally so, not always on reality. This was true for the attitudes of non-Leavenworth senior officers, junior officers too young to have attended the schools, and for the self-perception of Leavenworth men as well. According to one graduate, assigned from 1908 to 1910 at West Point, because the leadership at the academy was unsympathetic, the schools were out of favor at the Military Academy.[19] Consequently recent West Point graduates, selected to be among the elite of the professional army, sometimes first heard of Leavenworth when officers from their regiments were sent to the schools. But these young men looked upon the Leavenworth graduates with envy and respect. Officers such as Harold B. Fiske and Lorrin T. Richardson had prestige within their regiments "far above that associated with rank and seniority."[20] They were good practical officers, excellent instructors in the garrison school, and usually took an interest in the professional development of subordinates. Richardson, for example, encouraged Lieutenant Howard Davidson to read Griepenkerl's book and attempt a "do-it-yourself" course in tactical problem solving.[21]

Senior officers were not always as sympathetic to or awed by the Leavenworth men. Admittedly not everything learned at

Leavenworth was applicable to the garrison life and small-unit
actions characteristic of the Old Army. But many graduates
thought they were not given an opportunity to apply anything
they had learned that was applicable. In some cases they were
discouraged from doing so. Lieutenant colonels and colonels
who lacked postgraduate military education were most often
the inhibitors. The isolation, autonomy, and absolute authority
of the regimental and post commanders, combined with their
negative attitude, could have a deadening impact on the professional development of young officers. This negativism was
manifest toward graduates within their regiment by opposition
to their ideas, indifference to their accomplishments, sarcasm,
and jealousy. A 1904 graduate wrote of his experience at a
small western post:

> The Commanding Officer, a man of considerable ex-
> perience and many years service, and the second ranking
> officer, about to become a major, are both looking for-
> ward only to the time when they can retire from the serv-
> ice. Fixed in their mental habits, slow to assimilate new
> ideas and critical of everything different from the methods
> of the "old army," these officers have a marked (expressed)
> tendency to decry and belittle the modern methods and
> initiative shown by young officers.[22]

Although Howard Donnelly was too young to attend the prewar Leavenworth, he sympathized with the objectives of the
schools. At his first duty station, the Seventeenth Infantry in
Texas, he found a "general feeling of resentment and sarcasm
toward Leavenworth." Donnelly thought this was because most
of the regimental officers were over forty, had combat experience in the Spanish War and the Philippines, and, most importantly, were not themselves graduates.[23] They believed their age
and lack of school experience cut them off from further advancement. On the other hand, Leavenworth men by this time
were getting attention, choice assignments, and good prospects
for advancement.

The reception graduates received in their regiments reflected the mixed attitude of the army toward the schools. Some of the army's perceptions were clearly misperceptions, but other negative attitudes had a basis in fact. Undoubtedly there were graduates who could "repeat, page by page, all the books of the learned Leavenworth lieutenants and yet were helpless on the drill ground."[24] Even George Van Horn Moseley, an honor graduate and epitome of the school-trained officer, considered another graduate, John M. Palmer, a good writer but "not a practical soldier."[25] Because the schools tried to emphasize practical problem solving, such graduates were exceptions, however. Despite efforts to combat the reputation of Leavenworth as a "mere specking academy," stories that only good memorizers were the top graduates persisted. More damaging to Leavenworth's reputation than these misperceptions were the negative attitudes based on jealousy and resentment.

Some of the responsibility for negative attitudes toward the school lay with the graduates and other Leavenworth proponents. There were those who had made "such foolish pretensions in behalf of the schools that they have aroused a very natural and just antagonism in the service."[26] Graduates were really no wiser for having gone to Leavenworth and only slightly smarter. Their real advantage was in having had the opportunity to study and practice their professional responsibilities as tacticians and general staff officers.

Nevertheless, because of this opportunity Leavenworth graduates were a small, exclusive group of professionals who shared an experience that set them apart from, and above, their peers. They were interested in their fellow graduates, the school, and the military as a developing profession and discovered that because of this shared experience and the similar professional outlook, "one's friends were apt to be Leavenworth graduates."[27]

To some extent there was a generation gap between the older officers who were a product of the Indian-fighting army and the younger, school-trained Leavenworth men. Because their professional experiences had been different, it is not surprising that many in these two groups had very different ideas on important military issues of the day—the role of the General Staff, the importance of military education, the proper organization of the army. But it is easy to overemphasize this generation gap. Age alone did not determine an officer's attitude toward professionalization, reform, and modernization. Indeed the young Leavenworth men could succeed only to the extent that those senior to them in the chain of command encouraged, tolerated, or protected them. Bell is the most obvious example of this, but there were others, such as Hunter Liggett in the infantry and Joseph T. Dickman in the cavalry. Many of the older officers did not wholly agree with or understand what the young men were attempting, but they vaguely recognized that it was important for the army's future and consequently acquiesced.

Not all progressive-minded officers were young or even Leavenworth graduates, of course. Robert L. Bullard, West Point class of 1885 and a lieutenant colonel in 1910, read, thought, and wrote about the deficiencies in leadership, tactics, and training he had witnessed on active service in the Philippines. Bullard believed that to overcome these difficulties required a major intellectual effort on the part of all officers. Yet he was skeptical that the theoretical training provided at Leavenworth was the answer because it was too precise, too scientific, too impressed with German military methods and doctrine and not concerned enough with the problems of leadership, psychology, and human relations. Later, after a brief tour at Leavenworth, Bullard modified his view regarding the value of the schools. Although Bullard was never a Leavenworth man or even an enthusiastic supporter of the schools, he was among the more progressive-minded officers of that era.[28]

For many Leavenworth represented true professionalism because the schools had stimulated discussion of professional subjects throughout the army. By the time of World War I officers had come to expect Leavenworth to set the standards and be the final arbiter of tactical methods and doctrine.[29] Authorities at the schools encouraged these expectations and believed that Leavenworth's good reputation stemmed at least in part from "going beyond our legitimate work (narrowly construed) and doing things for individual officers and for the other departments of the government."[30] Other army schools, as well as individual Regular and militia officers, relied on Leavenworth for instructional materials and for guidance in interpreting the latest army doctrine.

Beginning about 1905 professional military periodicals, particularly *Cavalry Journal* and *Infantry Journal,* in each issue published tactical problems prepared for the courses at Leavenworth; the succeeding issue contained a solution. Thus officers not attending the schools could practice Leavenworth methods and compare their prowess to what the school expected of its students. In 1907 Morrison went a step further when he had the Army Service School Press print copies of problems, lectures, maps, and other instructional material and made available to all requesting them. Officers on the mailing list could buy the American and European textbooks used at the schools at a reduced rate. After one year about 500 officers were on this list; by 1915 the number had grown to 4,000.[31]

At least some officers found these materials professionally valuable. John J. Pershing followed the Leavenworth course through the mailing list and used the applicatory method as the basis for tactical instruction of troops he commanded.[32] Another future AEF commander and non-Leavenworth graduate, Charles P. Summerall, learned school methodology and doctrine from Charles D. Herron while they served together as instructors at West Point.[33] Still other officers studied "the Leavenworth way" while serving with the units assigned to the fort. Hunter Liggett, First Army commander in the AEF, "managed to assimilate most of what the School of the Line and the School of the Staff [Staff College] had to offer" when he spent two years with the Thirteenth Infantry. Ligget attended lectures, problems, and war games and read widely in the literature assigned for the course. Two years later he applied what he had learned as an instructor at the Army War College.[34] There were opportunities for nongraduates to assimilate what was taught at Leavenworth. That many utilized the opportunities indicated the importance they placed on the school. Spreading knowledge, doctrine, and methodology beyond the small group of graduates considerably increased the school's value.

Eventually the War Department institutionalized the process by which older officers learned Leavenworth doctrine and methods. For six weeks in 1908 and for three months each winter from 1911 to 1916, the department sent a group of field officers (majors, lieutenant colonels, and colonels) to Leavenworth for a special course in military art. The program had several objectives. Most importantly it introduced senior officers to the school, its program, its students, and its doctrine and created a more sympathetic atmosphere for Leavenworth within the army. It was also helpful to the senior officers because many were potential War College students and General Staff officers, who, because of rank and age, were ineligible for the normal School of the Line and Staff College tours. Morrison first proposed these classes to extend the usefulness of the schools and to promote uniformity of tactical doctrine.[35]

A group of six officers began a special six-week tactical course under Morrison's direction on September 1, 1908. The course concentrated on two familiar Leavenworth texts, *Studies in Minor Tactics*, and Griepenkerl's *Letters in Applied Tactics* and included thirty-eight map problems and war games. Because of the amount of work crammed into the six weeks, the students were dubbed the "Get Rich Quick" class. The immediate purpose of the 1908 course was to prepare these officers for the Army War College; all graduated from that institution in 1909.[36] Members of that and subsequent special classes were experienced officers who understood strategy and tactics. What they lacked, both individually and as a group, was the systematic approach to solving tactical and strategical problems as taught at Leavenworth and an appreciation of the role of general staff officers in planning and conducting military operations.

Despite obvious benefits to the service and the students, and for unexplained reasons, the War Department sent no special classes to Leavenworth in 1909 or 1910. In 1910 interest in the course revived. Officers at Leavenworth continued to favor it; one student in the 1908 special class published an article advocating continuation of the course;[37] an inspector general expressed approval;[38] finally, Hunter Liggett, then at the War Col-

lege, added his approval. He was also aware that a greater homogeneity of instruction methods and tactical doctrine was needed
among the students attending the War College.[39] Reviving the
special class was the easiest means of achieving that. Chief of
Staff Leonard Wood and Secretary of War Jacob M. Dickinson
agreed.[40] They not only ordered a special field officer class for
1911 but also invited the commandant of the Marine Corps to
send marine officers selected for the War College to this special
course.[41]

For the next six years the special class met from each January to March. Just over a hundred officers attended, including
five from the National Guard and eight from the Marine Corps.
The students were not graded although the Leavenworth faculty
reported on each student's suitability for the Army War College; about half of each class went to that institution. The
curriculum was similar to that of the first year: "The work was
almost entirely tactical and extended from a patrol to a division." Some historical work, including preparation of an original essay, and conferences on weapons and munitions were
added.[42] For students the schedule was full. In 1911 Robert
L. Bullard had time for little more than sleeping, eating, and
studying. The result, for Bullard, was "profitable enough."
At the end of the course he reflected: "From my 3 months at
Fort Leavenworth I derived three benefits: 1. Studied tactical
problems which I had neglected. 2. I improved in map reading.
3. Learned again what it means to work really."[43]

Although some officers apparently benefited from the field
officers' course, in 1916 the War College reported that its students who had taken the "Get Rich Quick" course had little
advantage at the college over those who had not.[44] But Leavenworth had gained from the experience. Leavenworth impressed
the field officers, who generally came away sympathetic to the
schools. One observer wrote of a fictitious Colonel Shellback
who constantly criticized Leavenworth and its graduates until
he attended the special class and returned to his post "convinced."[45]

At least a few Leavenworth people were not so impressed
with the motivation of all those attending the field officers'

course. They believed the short course was being used as a
shortcut to the Army War College by officers unwilling and
incapable of submitting to the rigors of the School of the Line
and the Staff College. Not just senior field officers had attended
the special course; several junior majors and at least one captain had also. When graduates of the special course received pro-
portionately more appointments (fifty of ninety-seven Regular
Army officers) to the War College after their six to ten weeks
of instruction than did Leavenworth graduates (only seven from
1904 to 1916) after their two years, the cause of the resentment was apparent, particularly since graduation from the Staff
College was supposed to be a natural stepping-stone to the War
College. Two chiefs of staff, Leonard Wood and Hugh L. Scott,
had to issue statements reiterating the purpose of the short
course to quiet criticism from the Leavenworth people, which
one observer described as "intense and bitter."[46] Scott affirmed
that the special course was not to be a short route to the War
College. Officers selected for that course were to be of exceptional ability and were too senior to have attended Leavenworth.[47] According to Wood, the course was not even a pre-
paratory class for the War College but was designed "to ac-
quaint field officers with methods of instruction at the service schools and thereby to facilitate the coordination of instruction throughout the service."[48]

The matter of the short course as a shortcut clearly exposed
Leavenworth's failure to fulfill a major role for which it had
been established. Responsibility for this failure lay principally
with the War Department, not with the authorities at the
schools. Only twenty post-1900 graduates served on the War
Department General Staff before 1917, 10 percent of the total
(see appendixes 4 and 5). Yet Root, Carter, and the other crea-
tors of the General Staff had wanted school-trained officers.
Selection boards turned elsewhere, much to the disgust of the
Leavenworth people, who had believed that attendance at the
schools would be the system of selection by which officers
qualified for appointment to the General Staff. Those selected
were usually able men but had no knowledge of the historic
origins of the General Staff, lacked an appreciation of general

staff officers as a separate professional type, and regarded the War Department General Staff as a superadministrative agency.

As John McAuley Palmer, one of the early General Staff officers, a graduate of Leavenworth, and the first real American student of the general staff concept, recognized, the entire problem stemmed from a failure to appreciate that two organizations had been created in 1903: the Office of the Chief of Staff and the War Department General Staff. The former should have assisted the Chief of Staff in coordinating, administering, and supervising the army; the latter should have prepared plans for the employment of the army in wartime. Because it was not general in the sense of being universal, the War Department General Staff was misnamed. A more proper designation would have been "generalship staff," or "operational staff," or "strategic staff," or "troop leading staff" because its sole task was to prepare the army for its primary function: fighting. Nearly all European armies kept these functions separate, with the war office or war ministry involved in day-to-day army administration and the general staff concerned exclusively with matters of tactics, strategy, and peacetime training of the service. Eligibility for duty on the general staff in these armies was by means of a vigorous process of education and elimination, the basis of which, in the German Army in particular, was the applicatory method of solving tactical problems. Because the general staff was supposed to be concerned with the principal professional military function, "the management of violence," general staff officers were trained to assist in leading a force of all arms, to understand the interrelationship of the several components to the tactical team, and to issue correct orders to such a tactical team in any military situation. Rigorous training, spirited competition among those eligible, elimination of those who did not measure up, and careful interchange between staff and command positions throughout a career prepared officers for this duty. As a measuring rod of their prowess, the applicatory method was used to test the relative ability of the potential general staff officers and eventually to determine who was eligible for the choice command and general staff positions.[49]

In the United States Army there was no rigorous process of

selection, no determination of eligibility, and little formal
general staff education. As a consequence the true general staff
function was ignored, and members of the War Department
General Staff became involved almost exclusively with supervising, coordinating, and administering routine army affairs,
which the Office of the Chief of Staff alone should have done.
Leavenworth and the War College were largely bypassed. Fewer
than half of all officers who served on the War Department
General Staff from 1903 through 1916 had attended advanced
military school. More important than attendance at a school
was the ability to perform operational staff functions, which
could easily be measured by the applicatory method. Schools
only formalized the learning process and provided an opportunity for practice. Unfortunately the War Department had no
rigorous selection process and did not establish a General Staff
eligibility list until after World War I. As a result of this mis-
reading of the General Staff legislation of 1903, Leavenworth
did not fulfill its potential as a professionalizing institution in
the army.

Despite this major shortcoming, Leavenworth tried to be a
center of intellectual activity and attempted to be of service to
the rest of the army. Officers at the schools were active in advocating legislation of value to the service and in serving as a
forum in which proposals before the General Staff were discussed, analyzed, refined, and returned to the War Department for further consideration. During 1909 and 1910, for
instance, the Army Service Schools branch of the Infantry
Association tried to reduce interbranch rivalry by proposing
a single promotion list for all Regular officers rather than the
separate branch lists, which tended to pit each branch against
all others to secure the largest share of any increase in the size
of the officer corps. A single list gave no branch unfair advantage. Although the single list was not adopted until 1916, the
issue forced officers to take a broader point of view and consider more than parochial branch interests.[50]

Officers on the War Department General Staff sought advice and guidance from students and instructors at Leavenworth
when preparing a study, "Organization of the Land Forces of

the United States," which was meant to become the basis of
future military legislation. The dialogue ranged from a discussion of what would be the best organization and geographical
disposition of the Regular Army, to what was the proper relationship between the Regulars and the National Guard, to
what was politically palatable to the rest of the army and to
the Congress.[51] As with the single list, this staff study had no
immediate impact; it was simply a policy statement, albeit a
significant one because it moved away from the strictly Uptonian position that previously had characterized most of professional military thought. From the perspective of the schools
it was significant because the General Staff had enough respect
for the professional opinions of Leavenworth men to consult
them and consider their views before submitting the final report. Because of the flexibility inherent in the course, particularly at the Staff College, Leavenworth was able to contribute
both to this study and to the proposal for a single list.

The most enduring contribution of Leavenworth to the pre-
World War I army was *Field Service Regulations.* In 1905 Captain Joseph T. Dickman, then on the General Staff and previously a tactics instructor at Leavenworth, prepared the first
American edition of this "military bible" by adapting the German Army regulations to American organization. Independent
of Dickman's effort, General Bell at Leavenworth recognized
the need for an authoritative tactical text that "would meet
the necessities of the competitive system of instruction" at the
schools. No single text had proved to be the definitive work on
which instructors could rely, particularly in grading tactical
problems. If instructors graded according to one book, the
students would claim their answer had been based on another.
Even after publication of the 1905 War Department edition,
Bell directed Major Daniel H. Boughton, the senior military
art instructor, to continue work on *Field Service Regulations*
adapted to the needs of Leavenworth. Although Bell left for
Washington and the General Staff in 1906 and Boughton joined
him there two years later, the work at Leavenworth on the revised regulations continued in earnest. Boughton, who remained
in charge of the project until final publication by the War De-

partment in 1910, submitted every page of the revised regulations to instructors and students at Leavenworth for study and
critical examination before its final form was approved. At the
schools, portions of the regulations were printed and used in
pamphlet form by students in solving tactical problems. Based
on this experience further revisions were made and returned
to Boughton and Bell, who considered each Leavenworth
change, often returning a draft to the schools for additional
modification. No wonder it was with some pride that Bell
claimed: "I don't believe that more careful consideration was
ever given to any manuscript or text book than was given to
this. It occupied at least five years in its production."[52]

Leavenworth played a prominent part in the production
of the 1910 *Field Service Regulations*, which became a comprehensive guide to the organization, administration, and tactics governing the army in the field. The needs of the school
precipitated the project; Leavenworth men (Bell and Boughton)
supervised it; students and instructors contributed data to the
refined final product. With only minor revisions in 1914 and
1918, the regulations stood the test of time and were the basis
of American field operations in France during World War I.
The 1910 *Field Service Regulations* was testament to Leavenworth's role as an intellectual center of the army.

The Leavenworth schools were not the only professionalizing
influence on the army in the early twentieth century. Officers
who served as professors of military science and tactics learned
from the civilians with whom they associated. The Cuban oc-
cupation of 1906 taught the General Staff numerous lessons
about organizing, mobilizing, and transporting large bodies of
troops. Officers such as John J. Pershing, James G. Harbord,
and Robert L. Bullard benefited as much from their service in
the Philippines as George Marshall, Malin Craig, and Fox Conner did from Leavenworth. American officers had more contact with foreign armies during these years than previously.
Several had been observers or attachés in the Russo-Japanese
and Boer wars. Others returned from their tours in the Philippines by way of Asia and Europe. In all these situations officers could learn more about their profession.

Leavenworth's contribution was to institutionalize and perpetuate the professionalizing process. Besides purveying common doctrine and instruction methods, it was a unifying influence on the army. Line officers learned the importance of staff work. Officers of the administrative staff and the general staff were introduced to problems of the line. And infantry, cavalry, and artillery officers discovered they all had common problems soluble only when they worked together. The schools consciously encouraged such cooperation. General Pershing declared that before World War I "joint service at the Leavenworth schools" was the chief factor in combating the jealousies, misunderstandings, and lack of common tactical doctrine.[53] Through the mailing list, articles in the service journals, and the efforts of graduates in their regiments, as instructors at garrison schools, and in major projects such as the production of the 1910 *Field Service Regulations*, Leavenworth successfully imparted these ideas to the rest of the army. For the long-range development of military professionalism, this was particularly important. It was essential to success during World War I.

From the turn of the century to America's entry into World War I, the Leavenworth schools served as an intellectual center of the army. They enjoyed a reputation far and above other army schools of the era, including the War College. The fact of being a Leavenworth man served as a measuring rod of an officer's professional prowess. Among graduates there was a corporate feeling, a sense of pride, not found among graduates of other army schools. Officers did not speak of "War College men," or "Riley men," or "Monroe men" as they did of "Leavenworth men."

Even though graduates had achieved a position of respect in the Regular Army before 1917, even though they were better trained than most of their peers, even though the schools had gone beyond their narrowly defined purposes to provide additional services for officers and the army, even though the schools and the officer corps were considerably better than before 1898, and even though progressive officers recognized all these facts and considered Leavenworth very important, other factors continued to limit Leavenworth's impact on the

army. In some circles graduates were ignored. More importantly, the number of graduates remained relatively small when
compared to the total officer corps. In 1919 the General Staff
reported that the principal fault of all the service schools before the war was their small capacity. The staff report concluded that as the number of graduates had increased, the impact of the schools was "becoming very marked."[54] The success of Leavenworth graduates in the American war effort,
particularly in the AEF, was very marked.

NOTES

1. Bell to Adjutant General, January 30, 1905, file 537, Record
Group 393, National Archives; ibid., March 16, 1905, file 990754, RG 94.
2. "Report of the Acting Commandant" (Burnham), 1914, RG 94.
3. Bell to Capt. H. S. Haight, December 2, 1905, file 596, RG 393;
Maj. Gen. W. W. Wotherspoon to Chief of Staff, May 19, 1913, file 7428,
Records of the Chief of Staff (1907-16), RG 165.
4. Capt. Chas. Danforth to Secretary, April 12, 1915, file 663, RG
393.
The detached service law, passed by Congress in 1912, was popularly
known as the Manchu Law. It sought to limit the amount of detached
service an officer could have and was aimed at reducing the influence of
the War Department General Staff.
5. Lt. Wm. E. Hunt to Secretary, June 7, 1905, file 693, RG 393.
6. Maj. Wm. A. Mann to Secretary General Staff, September 28,
1906, report 145, 3d Division General Staff, RG 165.
7. Chief of Division of Militia Affairs to Chief of Staff, April 8,
1913, file 2032372, RG 94.
8. Pershing memorandum, n.d. (circa 1929), general correspondence,
box 67, John J. Pershing Papers, Library of Congress.
9. Capt. R. M. Brambila to Secretary, September 14, 1906, file 5341,
RG 393.
10. L. M. Nuttman to author, December 16, 1971.
11. Chronological file, 1911, box 1, and chapter notes, vol. 5, box 16,
John McAuley Palmer Papers, Library of Congress.
12. Maj. Gen. Howard C. Davidson quoted in "Comments by Members
of the A.E.F.," in William Geffen, ed., *Command and Commanders in
Modern Warfare: Proceedings of the Second Military History Symposium,*

U.S. Air Force Academy (Washington, D.C.: GPO, 1969), pp. 63-64.

13. Perry L. Miles, *Fallen Leaves: Memories of an Old Soldier* (Berkeley, Calif.: Wuerth Publishing Co., 1961), p. 229.

14. Charles D. Herron to author, March 28, 1970; General of the Army Omar Bradley quoted in Geffen, *Command and Commanders*, p. 72.

15. Maj. Gen. Leroy H. Watson quoted in ibid., p. 74.

16. Donald Smythe, *Guerilla Warrior: The Early Life of John J. Pershing* (New York: Charles Scribner's Sons, 1973), pp. 256-60.

17. Richard H. McMaster, diary, November 1910, South Carolinia Library, University of South Carolina; Colonel Thomas A. Monroe quoted in William Geffen, "The Leavenworth Clique: A Military View," in Geffen, *Command and Commanders*, p. 57 n.15.

18. Chitty to Secretary, January 19, 1911, file 5001, RG 393.

19. Herron to author, March 28, 1970.

20. Geffen, "The Leavenworth Clique," pp. 51-52, esp. nn. 15, 18, 19.

21. Davidson statement in Geffen, *Command and Commanders*, p. 63.

22. Lt. W. E. Hunt to Secretary, June 7, 1905, file 693, RG 393.

23. Col. Howard Donnelly statement in Geffen, *Command and Commanders*, pp. 77-78.

24. G. S. Anderson, "Practical Military Instruction," *Journal of the Military Service Institution* 47 (November-December 1910): 334.

25. Note by Moseley on Palmer to Moseley, August 20, 1916, scrapbook of selected papers (1899-1942), George Van Horn Moseley Papers, Library of Congress.

26. John M. Palmer to Secretary A. W. C., February 19, 1914, War College Division File 8213-49, RG 165.

27. Herron to author, March 28, 1970.

28. Allan R. Millett, *The General: Robert L. Bullard and Officership in the United States Army* (Westport, Conn.: Greenwood Press, 1975), pp. 189-234.

29. See, for instance, Commandant Mounted Service School to Secretary A. W. C., January 9, 1914, WCD 8213-7, RG 165.

30. Secretary to Capt. C. D. Rhodes, January 24, 1911, file 537, RG 393.

31. "Report of the Assistant Commandant" (Morrison), in "Annual Report," 1908; "Annual Report of the Commandant" (H. A. Greene), 1915, RG 94.

32. John McAuley Palmer, *Washington, Lincoln, and Wilson: Three War Leaders* (Garden City, N. Y.: Doubleday, Doran, and Co., 1930), p. 298.

33. Herron to author, March 28, 1970.

34. Hunter Liggett, *A.E.F.: Ten Years Ago in France* (New York: Dodd, Mead, and Co., 1928), p. 288.

35. "Report of the Assistant Commandant" (Morrison), in "Annual Report," 1908, RG 94.

36. "Report of the Senior Instructor in Military Art, SOL" (Morrison), in "Annual Report of the Commandant," 1909, RG 94; list of lessons and exercises, special course, 1908-1909, misc. file, RG 393; Beaumont B. Buck, *Memories of Peace and War* (San Antonio: Naylor Co., 1935), p. 119.

37. Walter K. Wright, "Instruction of Officers in the Art of War," *Infantry Journal* 5 (January 1909): 495.

38. Lt. Col. C. G. Morton to Commandant, June 3, 1910, file 7274, RG 393.

39. Liggett to Secretary Army War College, file 1687243, RG 94.

40. Wood to Secretary of War, December 20, 1910, file 1727928, RG 94.

41. Secretary of War to Secretary of the Navy, December 29, 1910, file 1727928, RG 94.

42. "Report of the Senior Instructor in Military Art, Army Service Schools" (Morrison), in "Annual Report of the Commandant," 1911, RG 94.

43. Diary book no. 5, January 22, February 4, 17, April 3, 1911, Robert L. Bullard Papers, Library of Congress.

44. Brig. Gen. M. M. Macomb to Chief of Staff, February 21, 1916, file 12124, Chief of Staff Records (1907-1916), RG 165.

45. R. W. Ritchie, "Graduate School of War," *Harpers* 132 (February 1916): 456.

46. Maj. Farrand Sayre to Acting Commandant, March 19, 1913, file 2021476, RG 94.

47. Chief of Staff to Adjutant General, March 16, 1914, file 2134961, RG 94.

48. Office of the Chief of Staff Official Bulletin, April 4, 1914, file 2271588, RG 94.

49. Statement of John McAuley Palmer in *The National Defense: Hearings before the House Committee on Military Affairs*, 69th Cong., 2d sess., 1927, pp. 341-56; Palmer to Chief of Staff, November 21, 1916, WCD 639-136, RG 165; Palmer to Secretary A. W. C., February 19, 1914, WCD 8213-49, RG 165.

50. Chapter notes, vol. 5, box 16, Palmer Papers.

51. Chronological file, 1912, box 1, Palmer Papers; Russell F. Weigley,

History of the United States Army (New York: Macmillan, 1967), pp. 339-40.

52. Bell to Wood, January 1, 27, 1914, box 76, Leonard Woods Papers, Library of Congress; Edgar Frank Raines, Jr., "Major General J. Franklin Bell and Military Reform: The Chief of Staff Years, 1906-1910" (Ph.D. diss., University of Wisconsin, 1976), pp. 470-75.

53. Pershing to Adjutant General, February 10, 1919, file 8213-84, WCD., RG 165.

54. Maj. Gen. W. G. Haan to Secretary of War, August 30, 1919, file 428, Chief of Staff Records (1917-1921), RG 165.

8

THE AMERICAN EXPEDITIONARY FORCES EXPERIENCE

Leavenworth graduates served on the War Department General Staff, in a variety of positions on the active operations conducted by the army between 1900 and 1917, and in important positions throughout the army's educational system. The schools' real influence, however, was not felt until World War I when graduates made significant contributions to the conduct of the war at the highest level, especially in the American Expeditionary Forces. One AEF veteran stated: "It was World War I that put Leavenworth on the map!"[1]

There were a number of reasons why the war secured for Leavenworth a prominent position in the army, while previous experience had not. Because of their training Leavenworth graduates were among the best qualified officers to plan, organize, train and staff a large expeditionary force. Pershing recognized this and placed Leavenworth men in important positions because the schools had taught them the proper functioning of a general staff, operational planning, teaching tactics, and simply coping with large numbers of troops. The performance, as measured by efficiency ratings, of Leavenworth graduates compared well with that of their non-Leavenworth peers. After the war Pershing and other senior officers publicized these facts and publicly acknowledged the contribution of school-trained officers. The public support and praise of the era's premier American soldier ensured Leavenworth of the recognition and acceptance it previously had not had.

When Pershing was organizing his expeditionary force in France during the summer of 1917, he faced numerous problems. One of the most pressing was to organize an adequate general staff. Five of the seven staff officers who accompanied him to France were Staff College graduates; a sixth, James G. Harbord, had graduated from the Infantry and Cavalry School in 1895. But this group was far too small. Out of necessity, Pershing turned to other school-trained officers. The commander-in-chief recognized that "our most highly trained officers as a rule came from the Staff College at Fort Leavenworth and from the Army War College." By the end of that summer the staff at general headquarters "included some of the most efficient and highly educated officers in [the] Army."[2] In the interim Pershing and his assistants sought and recruited Leavenworth men for the AEF general staff.

In one cablegram to the War Department Pershing requested by name twenty-seven officers for general staff duty; twenty-four were Leavenworth men. Units already in France were scoured for graduates. Early in July, Harbord, the chief of staff at general headquarters (GHQ), requested names of School of the Line and Staff College graduates from the commanding general of the First Division.[3] By September GHQ wanted the names of such officers as soon as they arrived in France at the base ports.[4] Charles D. Herron went to Europe commanding an artillery regiment. Soon after arriving he was pulled out of that command and transferred to general staff duty because he was a Leavenworth man. His was a common experience because "there were only a few [Leavenworth men] in those days."[5] But those few were employed to good advantage.

During the war twelve officers served at general headquarters as chief of staff, deputy chief of staff, and heads of the G-1 through G-5 staff sections.[6] Another officer was acting chief of the G-3 section for two months. Seven of these officers had graduated from both the School of the Line and the Staff College; Fox Conner was a Staff College graduate only; Harbord

graduated from Leavenworth before the Spanish War. The chief
of staff, McAndrew, and deputy chief of staff, Leroy Eltinge,
during the period of most active operations (May to November
1918) were Leavenworth men. So were all those who headed
the staff sections concerned with operations, supply, and training.[7] Only James A. Logan and Avery Andrews, the successive
G-1s, and Dennis Nolan, the G-2, had not been to Leavenworth.
In the summer and fall of 1917, when planning for the organization and employment of the AEF was in earnest, Leavenworth
men dominated the operations section at GHQ. A member of the
section at that time, Hugh Drum, wrote to his wife: "My Leavenworth training is standing me in good stead these days." All seven
officers in the operations section had been at Leavenworth with
Drum as instructors or students.[8] On September 25, 1917, Drum
and two of his colleagues, Fox Conner and Leroy Eltinge, submitted "A Strategical Study of the Employment of the A.E.F.
Against the Imperial Government" to General Pershing.[9] This
staff study became the basis for the strategic employment of
American troops in France. In many essentials it was similar
to strategic studies these officers had prepared while still students at the Staff College.

Leavenworth men also headed the G-5 training section at
Pershing's headquarters where they imparted Leavenworth
methods and doctrine to the AEF school system. Paul B.
Malone and Harold B. Fiske, the two successive chiefs of the
section, were Leavenworth men, as were James W. McAndrew,
first commandant of the AEF schools, Alfred W. Bjornstad,
first director of the AEF Staff College at Langres, and Kirby
Walker, first director of the AEF School of the Line. Fox Conner and Hugh Drum had originally prepared the entire "School
Project for American Expeditionary Forces," which outlined
training needs at all levels, for the infantrymen in the front
lines, the staff officers overseeing entire operations, and the
specialist troops supporting them. The essentials of their scheme
were implemented.[10]

Tempered by experience and by French and British influence, the ideas, techniques, and doctrine taught in the AEF
were similar to what Leavenworth had taught before the war.

This was particularly true at the Langres Staff College. Although most division chiefs of staff, as well as the chiefs and assistant chiefs of the corps and armies, were Leavenworth graduates, there were not nearly enough to fill all the general staff positions in the AEF. In an abbreviated, three-month imitation of Leavenworth, Langres tried to bridge this gap. Between November 1917 and December 1918 Langres graduated four classes totaling 537 officers. Initially the permanent instructors were French and British officers, but Americans gradually replaced them; during the fourth class only one foreign instructor was present. As a tie to tradition, the staff named the primary lecture room Sherman Hall, after the main academic building at Fort Leavenworth.

The course at Langres provided officers information on changing regulations and organization of the AEF staffs. Whereas Leavenworth gave its graduates a broad foundation, sound tactical principles, and a basic understanding of staff work, Langres provided more specific information geared to the tasks the officers would perform immediately after graduation. Each student specialized in one aspect of staff work. Early in each course instructors evaluated the students and selected them as specialists in administration, intelligence, or operations. When they graduated these officers were assigned to either G-1, G-2, G-3, or G-4 sections of the various AEF staffs. In the problem solving at Langres, the class worked in groups, each a model general staff, with students concentrating on those parts of the problem involving their specialty. About half of the work at the college was done by these sections. For all four classes the work was similar: fifteen to twenty map problems, lectures, conferences, demonstrations, and occasional tours of headquarters at the front to witness firsthand how staffs functioned. The course included lectures on the use of maps, staff organization, the division in the defensive, and liaison between infantry and aviators; conferences on duties of the staff with respect to training, military use of railways, conducting trench reliefs, and preparations for an offensive; and map problems on a division in the attack (open warfare), the move of a division by bus and road, a billeting scheme, and a plan of operations.[11]

The common lessons, themes, and doctrine espoused at Langres and other AEF schools, despite the French and English influence, were reminiscent of Leavenworth. Langres taught that preparation and hard, methodical, systematic thought was the way to solve tactical problems. As Fiske reminded the first class: "Military geniuses have many times been seen scattered all over the problem room at Leavenworth waiting in vain for the inspiration that never came."[12] An estimate of the situation, which considered the mission, the enemy, friendly forces, and the terrain, and resulted in a decision and orders, was the proper format for problem solving. Reacting to the several years of stalemate on the Western Front, AEF tactical doctrine stressed offensive combat. Whereas trench warfare required rehearsed routine, open warfare demanded initiative, resourcefulness, flexibility, and assumption of responsibility by the tactical leaders. Langres, like Leavenworth, tried to develop these characteristics among its graduates.

Of the AEF schools Langres was especially successful in accomplishing its mission. As early as January 1918 one observer reported: "Bjornstad has started an excellent staff college course and one that is well adapted to the practical problem of training staff officers for our larger units."[13] The doctrinal precedents of Leavenworth instruction, based on the applicatory method, and leadership, planning, and instruction by Leavenworth graduates were significant factors in the success of Langres.

To a surprising extent the offensive combat studied at Leavenworth before 1917 was like that conducted by the Americans in 1918. One student of the European military experience has declared: "All the theoretical study in the Kriegsakademie, the Ecole de Guerre, and the Staff College [the English Staff College at Camberley] had not prepared the military leaders to expect a war such as this, nor had it instructed them how to fight under these new conditions."[14] This was not entirely true of the United States. Unlike the other armies of the Western Front, the AEF did not experience the horror of the trenches, the stalemated bloodbaths, and battles of attrition such as Verdun, the Somme, Passchendaele, and Ypres. Compared to these battles AEF operations, even the slow-going one in the Meuse-Argonne during October 1918, were indeed fluid. Three years of attrition (wearing down all the combatants), the new weapons (gas, airplanes, and tanks), and the strategic plans of both sides determined that 1918 would be a year of movement on the Western Front. The conscious effort of General Pershing to stress open warfare and conduct offensive operations also contributed.

Although Pershing recognized American shortcomings in a number of areas and was willing to learn or borrow from the Allies to fill obvious needs, he was adamant that neither the French nor the British could contribute anything to the tactical doctrine or instruction of his troops. He believed that extensive trench warfare made the infantry of both armies poor skirmishers, reduced their reliance on the rifle, made them too reliant on artillery, and, most importantly, stultified their initiative and aggressiveness. Pershing's doctrine for open warfare affirmed the rifle and bayonet as the essential infantry weapons and declared that the only way to success in battle was through an aggressive offensive.[15]

AEF doctrine conformed to *Field Service Regulations* and the tactical teachings of Leavenworth. Commanders were admonished that in pressing an aggressive offensive, they should adopt flexible formations that made use of the terrain and supporting arms. Particularly in frontal assaults, fire superiority and formations in depth were required to carry the enemy position. Conventional wisdom in the AEF deemed that such assaults could be successful if conducted in strength on a sufficiently narrow front but that simultaneous advance against an entire hostile front was out of the question.[16] Early experience in offensive operations, however, did not go according to doctrine. Of the battles during the summer of 1918 a German intelligence officer surprisingly reported of the Americans: "Apparently little stress is laid on marksmanship." There had also been little noticeable command influence, particularly in coordinating the action of infantry and artillery. Even later, after St. Mihiel, the Germans considered American troops strong and brave but command arrangements weak. The Germans believed the Americans relied too closely on the planned scheme of attack and thus were unable to adjust to changing situations.[17]

Americans were equally critical of themselves. The G-5 section at GHQ continually analyzed perfomance and pointed out shortcomings. In early September 1918 a G-5 publication noted: "The principles enunciated [regarding offensive combat] are not yet receiving due application." Although frontal assaults had to be made in depth, in recent operations formations had been so dense that individuals were elbow to elbow. Formations habitually lacked flexibility, scouts were seldom used, supporting arms were improperly employed, and junior officers displayed little initiative. Criticisms by G-5 continued after St. Mihiel and the first week of the Argonne, but there had been improvements. The principal criticisms were that the troops lacked aggressiveness and that brigade and division headquarters were too far in the rear. By the time of the armistice G-5 was satisfied: "Rapid progress in the art of war was everywhere to be seen. Divisions were more mobile, formations less dense; suitable maneuvers in the attack were more often seen; and vastly better advantage was taken of cover. Commanders and staffs were generally more confident, and worked with greater sureness and dispatch."[18] Clearly the AEF learned to fight by fighting, not because of Pershing's insistence on "open warfare" or because the prewar Leavenworth had expounded the proper tactical doctrine.

Pershing's fear that the Allies lacked the knowledge and the will to undertake open warfare proved unfounded. During the 1918 summer and fall offensives, the French and British performed as well as the AEF and captured even more territory and prisoners. On the other hand, the commander-in-chief's attitude toward offensive warfare, as well as the unit training schedules, the program of instruction at AEF schools, analysis of American tactical performance prepared by Leavenworth men in the G-5 section at GHQ, and the leadership of division, brigade, and regimental commanders (5, 59, and 177, respectively, were Leavenworth graduates) contributed to the eventual improvement of the AEF's tactical prowess.

Detailed planning, careful logistical buildup, extensive staff work, explicitly written operations orders, and not very imaginative tactics characterized American operations as they had the previous instruction at Leavenworth. Graduates who manned the AEF staffs turned to ideas, methods, and tactics with which they were familiar. At Leavenworth they had learned how to move masses of men and equipment through difficult terrain to battle; they had learned how the staff and line should coordinate their activities to accomplish these feats; they had practiced writing clear orders, which allowed easy understanding of the objectives. In France, they did the same things, only more in earnest.

In October 1918 when John M. Palmer met with three corps chiefs of staff, all Staff College graduates, to discuss plans for an attack, he thought: "Except for an ominous rumble to the north of us, I might have thought that we were back at Leavenworth. It seemed just like a Staff College conference between the phases of one of the old map maneuvers. The technique and the talk were just the same"[19] In unexpected ways the similarities between Leavenworth and the AEF became apparent. During the American 1918 fall offensives, Leavenworth graduates were operating on familiar ground. The maps used in their Griepenkerl problems at the schools covered the area around Metz, which was the general area of the Meuse-Argonne offensive. Nearly every village, city, and prominent terrain feature in the area was familiar to them. George Marshall recalled a humerous incident involving a friend, Preston Brown, who during the Meuse-Argonne commanded the Third Division. Once when Marshall visited the front, Brown pointed to a woods, the Hopital Wald, in the division's sector. He said that on Griepenkerl problems at Leavenworth, he had so many difficulties in that woods and had been "cut" on it so much in his solutions that, now, at every opportunity, he turned the division artillery on the woods and shelled it. That was his revenge on Griepenkerl and the Metz map.[20]

Staff officers who planned, coordinated, and supervised the American operations were usually Leavenworth graduates. Although staff organization and nomenclature changed some-

what, the theory and doctrine remained as they had learned
at the school. According to doctrine, the commander outlined
the parameters of the problem, the staff presented a detailed
solution or alternate solutions, the commander accepted, rejected, or modified one of the proposed solutions, and finally
the staff supervised the implementation of the plan. In this
last phase, the commander, freed from administrative detail,
could concentrate on the important tactical decisions that had
to be made, could more closely supervise his subordinate commanders, and could visit the critical spots in the line to cajole,
inspire, or encourage his men. The 1917 edition of the army's
Staff Manual described the role of the chief of staff: "He re-
lieves the commander of much that is unimportant, and for
the proper performance of his duties must be permitted much
independence of action. In the name of the commander he co-
ordinates and controls the operations of the troops, and the
technical and administrative services. . . . He is responsible for
the whole working of the staff. . . ; and his powers of super-
vision and control in the commander's name are co-extensive
with this duty, and will be exercised to the extent he may deem
necessary to carry out the same."[21] For the system to work
properly it required of both commanders and staffs loyalty,
trust, understanding, and, above all, knowledge of how the
system was supposed to work.

Differences in experience, age, outlook, and knowledge
sometimes created difficulties. In contrast to the Leavenworth
staff officers, most AEF division commanders had had no formal general staff training. Of the twenty-six divisions that saw
action in France, only three did not have a Leavenworth graduate as chief of staff at one time or other. Yet only five Leavenworth men commanded divisions in active operations, and in
three of those cases they did not assume command until late
October, shortly before the armistice. The staff officers and
brigade and regimental commanders who were Leavenworth
men were sometimes contemptuous of the division and corps
commanders, who were not. After the war Robert Alexander
(School of the Line 1909, Staff College 1910) wrote of a division commander under whom he had served: "Prior to the

war his opportunities for the command of mobile troops had been extremely limited nor had he availed himself of the opportunity for professional improvement offered by the Fort Leavenworth schools."[22] For their part the older officers were often ignorant or skeptical of the role and ability of their young staff officers. Some resented "those chiefs of staff . . . who told you everything to do, where to go, and what to say."[23] Others, because they did not understand the proper relationship with their chief of staff, allowed the chiefs too much or not enough authority.

When Alfred W. Bjornstad, a brilliant but prickly, sometimes bullying, personality served as III Corps chief of staff under Major General Robert L. Bullard, he had considerable authority to act independently of the corps commander. He assumed even more responsibility for the operational control of the corps and almost entirely ran the corps staff himself. He distrusted the other members of the staff, particularly the operations section, because they were not trained staff officers and were not Leavenworth men. Under Bullard he routinely first issued operations orders in the name of the commander and then informed Bullard of what had transpired. Bullard did not particularly like this practice (and personally he disliked Bjornstad), but he did nothing about the situation. In mid-October John L. Hines took over the corps when Bullard went to the Second Army. The first time Bjornstad issued a corps operations order without first consulting the corps commander, Hines, a much stronger personality than Bullard, had Bjornstad replaced.[24] Leavenworth doctrine before the war was particularly ambiguous on how far a chief of staff could go in assuming responsibility from the commander.[25] It necessarily was a matter of the ability and personality of the officers concerned. The case of Bjornstad, Bullard, and Hines well illustrated the dangers of such ambiguous doctrine. Following World War I the army took steps to correct the ambiguity.

In 1922 Hanson Ely, then commandant at Leavenworth and who during the war had served both as the chief of staff and the commander of a division, warned students to beware of "staff command." Too many staff officers, assistant staff officers, and third assistant staff officers had given orders to regimental, brigade, and division commanders, either on their own authority or in the name of the commanding general. Under certain circumstances chiefs of staff could do such things, but lesser staff officers had no such authority. Ely recounted how some commanders permitted their staff officers to issue orders to sign the commander's name to communiqués without prior consultation. Other commanders dismissed staff officers who did that; Ely clearly had the III Corps in mind.[26]

During the war most commanders and staff officers learned to adjust to their respective roles. Many commanders did know how to use their staffs. One staff officer recalled hearing a division commander comment that the only time he did not listen to his chief of staff, a Leavenworth man, he got into a terrific "muddle."[27]

How a good commander and a good staff worked together depended in large measure on the personalities of the officers involved. As chief of staff of the Seventy-eighth Division, Charles D. Herron stayed at headquarters to "pull ends together" and keep "track of everything that [went] on," while the commander went to the front where the firing was heaviest to solve problems on the spot.[28] In the First Division, by contrast, George Marshall, assistant chief of staff for operations, constantly visited the front, "often riding horseback through areas where shells were falling, explaining patiently to lower commanders what they were to do and why." Marshall was also the most important member of the planning staff and "to a large extent [the division commander's] executive."[29] Because Marshall was more capable and more aggressive than most, he was given more responsibility and duties.

The personal relationship among Leavenworth graduates, so many of whom were on the important AEF staffs, was also significant. Dealing with another Leavenworth man, who if he was not a personal friend at least "spoke the same language," facilitated matters. Leavenworth men believed in the abilities of one another. As Herron put it: "In cooperating, especially when actually in the line and time was precious, it enormously facilitated business to be able to deal with officers who understood the Leavenworth terms, with all their implications, and language did not need to be explained."[30]

General staff officers at different levels, division, corps, army, or GHQ had considerably different perspectives on the same situation, despite their common background and training. A division was an integral, structured military organization concerned not only with fighting but with the supply, administrative, and personal needs of its troops. Higher headquarters were naturally concerned with much broader questions. Corps and army headquarters served as umbrellas under which any number of interchangeable divisions could fight. Division staff officers consequently focused inward, whereas staffs at the other levels focused on external problems. Such differences shocked George Marshall when in July 1918 he moved from the First Division to the operations section at GHQ, where he found "a different world." Concrete concerns like feeding, clothing, housing, transporting, and fighting the troops suddenly gave way to questions of ocean tonnage, ports of debarkation, construction of docks and depots, and relations with the Allies. In the division day-to-day concerns seemed most crucial—morale, health, supplies, hot food. More intimate contact with troops made the casualties personal tragedies. At corps, army, and GHQ casualties became impersonal statistics, comfort of the troops became secondary to operational success, and many of the most critical problems appeared as mere abstractions. Marshall touched the heart of the dilemma when he lamented: "Each man was living in his own little world, ignorant to a surprising degree of all that occurred elsewhere."[31]

Another persistent problem in the AEF was the remoteness of general staff officers from the combat troops, a situation that led to operations orders based on incomplete information, especially on the condition and capability of the troops to carry out the assigned mission. Consequently operational demands were made that could not be fulfilled.

The problem was not entirely one of physical distance. Both commanders and staff officers recognized the necessity of frequent trips to the front for a first-hand appreciation of conditions.[32] Such visits by no means overcame the problem or even the picture of staff officers, particularly the Leavenworth men, as "chessboard players" too used to study and paper armies to cope with actual troops.[33]

Unrealistic staff planning did not help to ameliorate the situation. For instance, in the St. Mihiel offensive the First Army staff never found a satisfactory method for breaching the enemy barbed wire. The plans called for pioneer and engineer troops to precede the infantry across no-man's land and make gaps in the wire with Bangelore torpedoes and wire cutters. This laborious work took considerable time, and at places along the front, the assault troops, impatient with waiting, managed to walk across portions of still intact wire. The First Army was fortunate; light enemy resistance permitted such an acrobatic expedient. Had the Germans not already begun a withdrawal and had they more strongly contested the St. Mihiel salient, this shortcoming in the army plan might have been revealed with murderous results.[34]

The press of the Meuse-Argonne offensive, coming on the heels of St. Mihiel, allowed no opportunity for critical analysis of the shortcomings of the operations plan and staff work in the earlier operation. Quite similar problems consequently arose in the objectives set for the Argonne assault. Success in that operation depended on the rapid seizure of the main German defensive position, the Kriemhilde Stellung, before enemy reinforcements could arrive. Drum and the First Army operations staff convinced themselves and General Pershing that it could be taken, despite rugged terrain, good German defensive dispositions, and several untried assault divisions. Because the plans originated with the First Army staff and because operations orders were initially discussed among the army, corps, and divisions staffs, not among the responsible commanders, the Leavenworth-trained staff officers must bear some responsibility for the eventual slowdown of the offensive.[35]

In the operational phase of the offensive, staff officers transmitted the intentions of the commanding general to lower echelons. From the standpoint of those receiving the orders, such staff officers became more than the transmitters of bad tidings.

Charles D. Rhodes (SOL 1907, SC 1908), attached to the Forty-second Division during the closing days of the war, harbored resentment toward the I Corps chief of staff, Malin Craig (SOL 1904, SC 1905), for pressuring the division to continue the pursuit toward Sedan "day and night without stopping." Craig had admonished the division for not having done this, despite its "awfully tired" troops and short rations.[36] How tactfully an officer transmitted such orders often determined how successfully the orders were carried out. Clearly difficulties in this area existed in the AEF where staff and the line had different perspectives of the same problem. Overall objectives of the operation concerned the staff, while problems of the individual troops became paramount for the line. No amount of Leavenworth education could have overcome this dichotomy.

Leavenworth men prepared the plans and executed exacting, complicated staff work connected with two major offensives—St. Mihiel and the Meuse-Argonne. Fox Conner (SC 1906) initially conceived the St. Mihiel operation. Planners from Conner's GHQ G-3 section, supervised by Marshall (SOL 1907, SC 1908) and Walter S. Grant (SOL 1914, SC 1915), drafted and revised most of the First Army's plans. As chief of staff of the First Army, Hugh Drum (SOL 1911, SC 1912) saw that the staff work at the army level went smoothly and that the army staff properly implemented the plan. Robert McCleave (SOL 1910, SC 1911), operations officer at First Army, and his section worked out the details of the plan. Marshall was largely responsible for the staff work necessary to shift the First Army's effort from the attack at St. Mihiel ninety degrees to the north for the assault in the Meuse-Argonne. Later Drum took Marshall from GHQ and made him chief of operations for the First Army. Their Leavenworth background, creating a common doctrine, language, and outlook, allowed these men to work well together.

For an offensive on the scale of St. Mihiel, the planning necessary to concentrate troops, supplies, equipment, and supporting arms at a single time and place to conduct the assault was a major undertaking. The G-3 section at First Army prepared the detailed march tables required to accomplish such a concentration. It is unlikely that officers without previous experience in so complex an endeavor could have successfully completed the work. The head of the G-3 section, McCleave, and his principal assistants were Leavenworth men. At the schools a considerable portion of the frequent map maneuvers had consisted of preparing march tables for just such an exercise in concentration. Such exercises had made them experienced staff officers.

Planning prior to the September 12 St. Mihiel attack was complicated further after September 2 when Foch announced his intentions for a subsequent American offensive in the Meuse-Argonne. The simultaneous staff work required to extract the First Army from its limited offensive against the St. Mihiel salient and shift its axis northward for a second, all-out offensive was overwhelming. That the army planners succeeded to the extent they did was miraculous, particularly in light of the obstacles they faced. From the time planning began in earnest, they had only ten days to work out all the details. About 220,000 troops had to be withdrawn from St. Mihiel and moved with an additional 600,000 into a narrow zone of operations. Only three roads, one for each corps, led into the proposed zone, and to maintain the security of the operation prior to the attack, these roads could be used only during darkness. Congestion along the three arteries was unavoidable, but the staff anticipated the problem and prepared expedients to lessen its impact. Although the planners were too optimistic in thinking that the attack could break the main German defense, nonetheless the concentration of troops for the Argonne went without a hitch, and the initial attack was far more successful than the skeptics had expected.

When the offensive bogged down early in October, disorganization in several of the assault divisions, not poor staff work, was the principal cause. Logistics support for the operation, despite the numerous obstacles, remained good, although at times Drum had to take draconian measures to ensure that ammunition reached the troops. During St. Mihiel and the Meuse-Argonne the Leavenworth men on the GHQ and army staffs did what they had been trained for. The staff work was not perfect but was more than satisfactory. Men like Marshall and Drum had performed brilliantly. In both operations, because Pershing was preoccupied with the morals and morale of his troops and with inter-Allied politics and strategy, Drum ran the First Army. It is not surprising that this was the case; he had been trained for the task. Drum spoke for the other Leavenworth men when he wrote to his wife: "All the hard hours of study at Leavenworth and those spent here have borne fruit and my reward is now at hand."[37]

No system of training can ensure that soldiers will succeed in combat. As Frederick Palmer, the war correspondent, observed of officers at all levels in the AEF:

> Regular as well as reserve officers who had never been in action were to prove again that no amount of study of the theory of war, invaluable as it was, may teach a man how to keep his head in handling a thousand or three thousand men under fire. West Point cadet drill, Philippine jungle and "paddy" dikes, Leavenworth Staff School, army post routine, and border service had no precedent of experience for the problems of maneuver which they now had to solve.[38]

But there was no doubt that Leavenworth training paid off, made a difference in how an officer performed, and was an improvement from previous wars. It was considerably more expensive in terms of casualties and money to train Ulysses Grant early in his Civil War career for the high command he later held than to train officers of the World War I generation in army schools.[39]

Evidence compiled shortly after the war indicated that as a group Leavenworth men performed better than officers who were not graduates. Late in 1918 General Pershing ordered efficiency ratings compiled on all general officers in the AEF. The most startling result was that of 180 brigadier generals rated, only twenty were in the highest category, "excellent," yet fourteen of those twenty were post-1900 graduates of Leav-

enworth. Of 48 generals rated "deficient," 4 were Leavenworth men, only 1 of whom had received good recommendations from the faculty upon graduation.[40] In another study
based on efficiency ratings, all School of the Line graduates
from 1903 through 1916 compared favorably to nongraduates.
The percentage of "below average" and "inferior" ratings was
nearly the same for both groups, while Leavenworth men had
a 10 percent advantage in the two highest ratings.[41] (See appendix 6.) Postgraduate military education clearly had its limitations. Average and good officers could be made better, but
inferior quality could not be improved. Education could not,
after all, instill character, courage, or even leadership.

One former AEF staff officer declared that after the war:
"There was no doubt in the Army as to the value of the
school."[42] The First Army commander, Hunter Liggett, agreed.
He thought Leavenworth men, "by virtue of their military education," were the "bulwark" of the staffs.[43] General Pershing
concurred: "I declare without hesitation that but for the training in General Staff duties given our officers at the Service
Schools, at home before the war and in France during the war,
our successful handling of great masses of partially trained
troops . . . could not have been possible."[44]

The massive effort required to support the American Expeditionary Forces an ocean away from the United States demanded careful staff work unique to that point in American
history. The tactical and strategical situation on the Western
Front, with mass conscript armies, new weapons, coalition
partners, and close integration in combat of several arms, was
different from previous American experience. General Harbord reflected: "It was a war of another age than the one in
which our fathers fought."[45] Despite the unique circumstances,
unlike 1898 there were no logistics debacles. Operational failures were minimal with no clear defeats or reverses, unlike the
Civil War. Yet there had been impressive successes that to a
large degree could be attributed to superb planning and coordination by Leavenworth-trained staff officers.

The AEF experience aptly reflected the strengths and limitations of officer education, specifically as conducted at Leaven-

worth. Personality remained an important ingredient of military leadership. Leavenworth had prepared its graduates to recognize the impact of personality in such areas as the relationship between a commander and his chief of staff but could not prevent personality clashes. That established doctrine did not always conform to reality was clear in the insistence on open warfare. Too much self-confidence, too great a belief in the rationality of warfare, and too high expectations of what the combat troops could accomplish by many of the Leavenworth staff officers compounded the problems that arose from the dichotomy between reality and doctrine. By means of the applicatory method, however, Leavenworth had trained its graduates in systematic planning and problem solving under pressure. In the AEF that is what they did, thus contributing significantly to the success of the American army.

NOTES

1. Maj. Gen. C. P. Gross quoted in "Comments by Members of the A.E.F.," in William Geffen, ed., *Command and Commanders in Modern Warfare: Proceedings of the Second Military History Symposium, U.S. Air Force Academy* (Washington, D.C.: GPO, 1969), p. 71.

2. John J. Pershing, *My Experiences in the World War* (New York: Frederick A. Stokes Co., 1931), 1:20, 103.

3. Harbord to Benj. Alvord (AEF Adjutant General), July 1, 1917, file 410, AEF Adjutant General Training File, Record Group 120, Records of the American Expeditionary Forces, National Archives.

4. Assistant Adjutant General to Commanding General, Line of Communication, September 29, 1917, AEF file 3154, RG 120.

5. Forrest C. Pogue interview with Charles D. Herron, May 28, 1958.

6. G-1 is the personnel and administrative section of the general staff; G-2 the intelligence section; G-3 the operations section; G-4 the supply section; and G-5 the training section.

7. Edward M. Coffman, "The American Military Generation Gap in World War I: The Leavenworth Clique in the A.E.F.," in Geffen, *Command and Commanders*, p. 37. For this and further descriptions of personnel matters in the AEF, I used *Commandants, Staff, Faculty, and Graduates, 1881-1926* (Fort Leavenworth: General Service Schools Press, 1926); *Order of Battle of the United States Land Forces in the World*

War: American Expeditionary Forces: General Headquarters, Armies,
Army Corps, Services of Supply, and Separate Forces (Washington, D.C.:
GPO, 1937); *Order of Battle of the United States Land Forces in the*
World War: American Expeditionary Forces: Divisions (Washington,
D.C.: GPO, 1931).

8. Drum quoted in Edward M. Coffman, *The War to End All Wars*
(New York: Oxford University Press, 1968), p. 125.

9. Strategical Study, file 683, G-3 Records, RG 120.

10. Reports to the commander-in-chief, AEF, file 215, RG 120.

11. "Training in the A.E.F.," box 3, Harold B. Fiske Papers, RG 200;
reports to the commander-in-chief, AEF, file 218, RG 120; schedule of
classes, file 95, Staff College Records, RG 120.

12. Fiske lecture, "Map Problems," December 7, 1917, file 15125-
30, AEF Adjutant General Records, RG 120.

13. Palmer to Harbord, January 22, 1918, file 11369, AEF Adjutant
General Records, RG 120.

14. Jay Luvaas, *The Military Legacy of the Civil War* (Chicago: University of Chicago Press, 1959), p. 203.

15. Pershing, *My Experiences*, 1:252, 254; Pershing to Adjutant General, cable 1630-s, August 27, 1918, RG 120.

16. War Department, *Field Service Regulations: Corrected to July 31,*
1918 (Washington, D.C.: GPO, 1918); "Memorandum for Corps and
Division Commanders: Training," August 5, 1918, GHQ, AEF, RG 120.

17. Section for Foreign Armies, "Report on American Training,"
July 31, 1918, file 801-21.8; Lt. Col. C. von Giehrl, "The Fight for St.
Mihiel," January 9, 1922, file 801-18.2, German World War I records,
RG 165.

18. "Combat Instructions," September 5, 1918, GHQ, AEF; "Notes
on Recent Operations: No. 3," October 12, 1918, GHQ, AEF; "Notes
on Recent Operations: No. 4," November 22, 1918, GHQ, AEF.

19. John McAuley Palmer, *Washington, Lincoln, and Wilson: Three*
War Leaders (Garden City, N.Y.: Doubleday, Doran, and Co., 1930),
p. 340.

20. Forest C. Pogue interview with George C. Marshall, April 4, 1957.
"Cut" was the term used at Leavenworth to describe points subtracted
from students' grades for mistakes made on solutions of practical problems.

21. War Department, *Staff Manual* (Washington, D.C.: GPO, 1917),
pp. 9-10.

22. Robert Alexander, *Memoirs of World War I* (New York: Macmillan, 1931), p. 66.

23. Arthur L. Conger, "The Military Education of Grant as General," *The Wisconsin Magazine of History* 4 (1921): 254.

24. Senate Committee on Military Affairs, *Hearings on the Nomination of Col. Alfred W. Bjornstad, U.S. Army, for Nomination to be a Brigadier General*, 68th Cong., 2d sess., 1925, pp. 16-17, 95-96.

25. J. W. McAndrew, "The Chief of Staff," *Infantry Journal* 9 (September-October 1912): 184, 214; this summary of Staff College doctrine states that no rigid rules could be made regarding the relationship between a Chief of Staff and a commander.

26. Hanson E. Ely, *Address at Opening of General Service Schools* (Fort Leavenworth: General Service Schools Press, 1922), pp. 11-12.

27. Conger, "Military Education of Grant," p. 259.

28. Coffman, *War to End All Wars*, p. 265.

29. Forrest C. Pogue, *George C. Marshall: Education of a General* (New York: Viking Press, 1963), p. 164.

30. Charles D. Herron to author, March 28, 1970.

31. George C. Marshall, *Memoirs of My Services in the World War*, ed. James L. Collins, Jr. (Boston: Houghton Mifflin, 1976), pp. 120-21.

32. Elliott L. Johnson, "The Military Experiences of Hugh A. Drum from 1898-1918" (Ph.D. diss., University of Wisconsin, 1975), pp. 256, 343.

33. Frederick Palmer, *Our Greatest Battle* (New York: Dodd, Mead, 1919), p. 439.

34. Marshall, *Memoirs*, pp. 134-36, 147.

35. Allan R. Millett, *The General: Robert L. Bullard and Officership in the United States Army, 1881-1925* (Westport, Conn.: Greenwood Press, 1975), pp. 398-400.

36. Charles D. Rhodes, "Diary Notes of a Soldier" (unpublished manuscript, National Archives Library), p. 72 in Chapter VIII.

37. Drum quoted in Coffman, *War to End All Wars*, p. 356; Pogue, *Education of a General*, pp. 169-89; Johnson, "Drum," pp. 289-359; Drum to Marshall, September 27, 1919, box 13, Pershing Papers, RG 200; Donald Smythe, "Venereal Disease: The A.E.F.'s Experience," *Prologue* 9 (Summer 1977): 65-74.

38. Palmer, *Greatest Battle*, p. 122.

39. Conger, "Military Education of Grant," p. 260.

40. General officer efficiency reports, file 19052-A-74, AEF Adjutant General Records, RG 120; class standings and academic board recommendations, file 6105, War College Division, RG 165.

41. "War Record of Leavenworth Graduates," *Infantry Journal* 20 (May 1922): 480-84; the study on which this article is based is filed

under AG 352.07 (9-8-21), bulky file, Records of the Adjutant General's Office, 1917-25, RG 407, National Archives.

42. Herron to author, March 28, 1970.

43. Hunter Liggett, *A.E.F.: Ten Years Ago in France* (New York: Dodd, Mead, 1928), p. 252.

44. Pershing quoted in Ely, *Address,* p. 9.

45. James G. Harbord, "A Year as Chief of Staff," lecture at Army War College, February 8, 1929, Army War College Records, RG 165.

APPENDIXES

Foreign Observations of Leavenworth

Just as Americans had shown interest in foreign military schools, between 1904 and 1916 a number of foreign officers visited Leavenworth, foreign attachés in Washington reported on the schools, and a few officers from Cuba and Mexico took the course. On at least thirteen occasions foreign military personnel visited the post: two visits by Australians, two by Germans, two by Japanese, two by Russians, and one each by Cubans, Chinese, Mexicans, New Zealanders, and Venezuelans.[1] Available evidence indicates that the school probably impressed most of the foreign visitors. Following a visit in 1909, Major General J. C. Hoad, inspector general of the Australian Army, commented on the "completeness and thoroughness of both theoretical and practical work." The quality of instruction and the industry, earnestness, and ability of the students were similarly impressive.[2] The conscientiousness and serious demeanor of students and instructors had also impressed a French military attaché who visited Leavenworth in 1905, even though, as he recognized, at this time the schools were still in a period of transition.[3]

With good reason other foreign observers had reservations about the quality of the American officer corps, indicating at least indirectly that they believed Leavenworth's impact was minimal. A number of British reports on the subject, in the midst of the Elihu Root reforms, reflected skepticism that the close attention to military education would reap benefits. The major handicap, they stated, was the lack of opportunity for senior American officers to exercise command of large formations.[4] On the eve of the American declaration of war in 1917, at least one German intelligence officer agreed. Although the American officer corps was well prepared in theoretical aspects of the profession, he thought practical instruction had been slight because troop leaders had never commanded units larger than battalions or regiments.[5]

These criticisms were to some extent correct but also irrelevant. Few American officers in 1905 or 1917 had had experience actually commanding brigades, much less divisions or army corps, but they did have active service campaigning in the Philippines and along the Mexican border. Besides, at the Army War College and at Leavenworth potential commanders and staff officers had been intellectually prepared, through means of map exercises and war games, to lead larger formations. The superficial analysis of American army education by the European critics had missed this point. American officers of the early twentieth century probably understood European armies better than the Europeans understood the American.

NOTES

1. Index entries "Foreign Officers" and "Visitors," Army Service Schools Correspondence, 1901-18, Records of U.S. Army Continental Commands, Record Group 393, National Archives.

2. Extract from report submitted by Major General J. C. Hoad, 1908-09, CRS, A1194, item 6710:20.15, Australian Archives, Kingston, Australia.

3. Captain Fournier to 2e Bureau, December 21, 1905, File 7N1713, Service historique de l'Armée, Vincennes, France. Fournier's report indicates he visited Fort Leavenworth, although Army Service Schools records contain no documentation on such a visit.

4. Intelligence Department, "Report on Changes in Foreign Armies in 1902," WO 106/292; Colonel H. J. Foster, Military Resources of the United States 1904, WO 33/327, A936; Colonel W. R. Robertson, Military Resources of the United States 1905, WO 106/40, B1/16; Public Record Office, London.

5. Nachrichten-Abteilung No. 3686a, April 4, 1917, AOK 2, German World War I Military Records, Records of the War Department General and Special Staffs, RG 165, National Archives.

APPENDIX 2

School of the Line Graduates by Rank and Branch

Year	Total	Major	Captain	First Lieutenant	Second Lieutenant	Cavalry	Infantry	Engineers	Field Artillery	Coast Artillery	Signal Corps
1905	43		11	30	2	16	27				
1906	45		12	21	12	15	29	1			
1907	38		10	15	13	13	22		3		
1908	39	1	36	2		10	27				2
1909	32		32			7	20		4		1
1910	36	1	35			6	26	1	3		
1911	33	3	30			8	20		5		
1912	46	2	44			13	28		5		
1913	22	1	21			7	10		2	3	
1914	40	1	24	15		13	24		1	2	
1915	30	3	27			9	16		3	2	
1916	28	3	25			7	18		1	2	
Total	432	15	307	83	27	124	267	2	27	9	3

APPENDIX 3

Staff College Graduates by Rank and Branch

Year	Total	Major	Captain	First Lieutenant	Second Lieutenant	Cavalry	Infantry	Engineers	Field Artillery	Quarter-master	Coast Artillery	Signal Corps
1905	23		13	8	2	8	10	2	3			
1906	23		12	10	1	9	9	2	3			
1907	18		7	11		6	10	1				1
1908	22		10	11	1	10	9		3			
1909	23		23			10	12					1
1910	21	2	19			5	12					1
1911	20[a]	1	19			3	14	1	1			
1912	24	3	19	2		6	14	2	2	1		
1913	14	2	12			4	7		3			
1914	19	2	17			5	8	2	2		2	
1915	21	2	14	5		6	12	2			1	
1916	23	2	21			7	9	2	3		2	
Total	251	14	186	47	4	79	126	14	23	1	5	3

[a]One did not graduate.

APPENDIX 4

Background of All Officers Serving on War Department General Staff,
1904-1916

Pre-1900	
Leavenworth graduates	13
Leavenworth and Army War College graduates	16
Post-1900	
Leavenworth graduates	13
Leavenworth and Army War College graduates	7
Army War College graduates only	41
No military postgraduate schooling	112
Total	202

Source: *Army Register*, 1904-1916

APPENDIX 5

All Captains and Majors Serving on War Department General Staff,
1904-1916

Pre-1900	
Leavenworth graduates	10
Leavenworth and Army War College graduates	15
Post-1900	
Leavenworth graduates	13
Leavenworth and Army War College graduates	7
Army War College graduates only	33
No military postgraduate schooling	67
Total	145

Source: *Army Register,* 1904-1916

APPENDIX 6

Duties and Performance of Leavenworth Graduates,
World War I

	Honor Graduates (N=67)	Distinguished Graduates (N=191)	Graduates (N=291)
Duties			
High command	28.3%	17.8%	5.1%
Command	31.3	31.9	37.6
General Staff	70.2	52.3	20.3
Administrative, technical, and supply staff	18	21.4	23.7
Performance			
Above average or superior	83.5	69.9	36.7
Average	9	26.8	49.5
Below average or inferior	5.5	3.3	13.8

	Above Average and Superior	Average	Below Average and Inferior
Field officers of the army	48.6%	44%	7.4%
All graduates, School of the Line	58.2	34.2	7.6

Note: Percentages amount to more than 100 because some officers held
more than one position and were thus listed in more than one
category.

Source: "War Record of Leavenworth Graduates," *Infantry Journal* 20
(May 1922): 482.

BIBLIOGRAPHICAL ESSAY

MILITARY PROFESSIONALISM, MILITARY EDUCATION, AND THE U.S. ARMY

The standard works on American military professionalism remain Samuel P. Huntington, *The Soldier and the State* (Cambridge: Harvard University Press, 1957), and Morris Janowitz, *The Professional Soldier* (Glencoe, Illinois: The Free Press, 1960), although some recent work has refined and revised their findings; see, for instance, William B. Skelton, "Professionalization in the U.S. Army Officer Corps during the Age of Jackson," *Armed Forces and Society* 1 (August 1975), and Allan R. Millett, *Military Professionalism and Officership in America: Mershon Center Briefing Paper Number Two* (Columbus, Ohio: The Mershon Center, 1977).

I found Laurence R. Veysey, *The Emergence of the American University* (Chicago: University of Chicago Press, 1965), a good summary of developments in American higher education, many of which paralleled the evolution of Leavenworth, during the late nineteenth and early twentieth centuries. Jurgen Herbst's analysis of the transfer of knowledge and culture from Germany to the United States, *The German Historical School in American Scholarship* (Ithaca: Cornell University Press, 1965), was especially applicable when studying how the American army learned from foreign armies.

Of the principal European staff colleges, only Camberley has a recent full-fledged history: Brian Bond, *The Victorian*

Army and the Staff College (London: Eyre Methuen, 1972).
This excellent study is very good in establishing the context
within which Camberley emerged during the nineteenth century. Herbert Rosinski, *The German Army* (Washington, D.C.:
Infantry Journal Press, 1944), presents a lively but brief analysis of the *Kriegsakademie*, while B. H. Liddell-Hart, *Foch:
Man of Orleans* (Boston: Little, Brown, 1932), includes a similar treatment of the *Ecole supérieure de guerre*.

The three major works of Russell F. Weigley—*The American
Way of War: A History of United States Strategy and Policy*
(New York: Macmillan, 1973), *History of the United States
Army* (New York: Macmillan, 1967), and *Towards an American
Army* (New York: Columbia University Press, 1962)—ably de-
scribe the intellectual and institutional basis of the United
States Army. The introductory chapters of Graham A. Cosmas,
*An Army for Empire: The United States Army and the Span-
ish American War* (Columbia: University of Missouri Press,
1971), are the best source for information on army reform
in the late nineteenth century. The interaction of technology,
bureaucracy, and professionalism in the U.S. Army is outlined
by Edgar F. Raines, Jr., "Major General J. Franklin Bell and
Military Reform: The Chief of Staff Years, 1906-1910" (Ph.D.
diss., University of Wisconsin, 1976). Bell's important role in
the development of Leavenworth made this an especially worthwhile source. Although not concerned with Leavenworth men,
two recent biographies helped me understand the peacetime
army at the turn of the century: Allan R. Millett, *The General:
Robert L. Bullard and Officership in the United States Army,
1881-1925* (Westport, Conn.: Greenwood Press, 1975), and
Heath Twichell, Jr., *Allen: The Biography of an Army Officer*
(New Brunswick, N.J.: Rutgers University Press, 1974).

PRINCIPAL SOURCES ON LEAVENWORTH

Annual reports of the commandant and War Department
General Orders both provided basic information on the purpose, organization, and curriculum of Leavenworth. Usually
the commandant's report included additional reports from the

heads of the academic departments describing in great detail the course content, instructional methods, and problems that had arisen during the previous year. Through 1908 the annual reports were included in the published *Annual Reports of the War Department*. Drafts of nearly all the annual reports from 1882 through 1916 were filed in the "annual report box" for each year, among the records of the Adjutant General's Office, Record Group 94, National Archives. Because the adjutant general was the office of record for the War Department, this record group also amply documented policy decisions on the establishment of the School of Application in 1881, subsequent changes in the organization and mission, and War Department support for the routine administration of the schools. For the period from 1903 to 1919, the correspondence of the War College Division, among the records of the War Department General Staff, Record Group 165, contained useful information on Leavenworth and the other service schools. There were also several excellent reports in this series, under files 639 and 8213, analyzing the army's educational system and the necessity for specially trained general staff officers.

The correspondence files of the Army Service Schools, Fort Leavenworth, Kansas, 1908-18, among the records of the U.S. Army Continental Commands, Record Group 393, amount to seventy-five archive boxes. Although it contained much routine, administrative correspondence, I examined the entire series, box by box, folder by folder. This proved a worthwhile exercise; I not only developed an appreciation for how military organizations functioned during the early twentieth century but uncovered valuable documentation reflecting the spirit, pride, and corporateness of the Leavenworth men. This was especially evident in letters to the school secretary from recent graduates.

LEAVENWORTH MEN

An examination of a number of unpublished memoirs, diaries, and manuscript collections, as well as interviews and correspondence with retired officers, provided insight into life at Leavenworth, how graduates regarded their Leavenworth training, and how valuable that training proved throughout an army career.

The diaries of Ola W. Bell (SOL 1915) at the West Point Library and Richard H. McMaster (SOL 1909, SC 1910, instructor 1911-12) at the South Carolinia Library included terse daily entries that vividly demonstrate the hard physical and mental effort required of the Leavenworth course. From these diaries and the Ernest Gose (SOL 1911, SC 1912) and Matthew F. Steele (instructor 1903-08) collections at the Military History Institute, Carlisle Barracks, Pennsylvania, I got a flavor of daily post routine, competition for the staff class, and social life at Leavenworth. Correspondence between graduates, often including comments on their experience at the schools, can be found in the papers of George Van Horn Moseley (SOL 1908, SC 1909) at the Library of Congress, Harold B. Fiske (SOL 1910, SC 1911, instructor 1911-12, 1915-16), at the National Archives, Walter Krueger (SOL 1906, SC 1907, instructor 1909-12) and Charles D. Rhodes (SOL 1907, SC 1908), both at West Point. The correspondence of John F. Morrison (instructor 1907-12) in the Charles Boardman papers at the State Historical Society of Wisconsin and of Eben Swift (instructor 1893-97, 1906-14, 1916) in the National Archives and Swift's unpublished memoir at West Point were good sources for information on two of the important instructors.

Although the papers of John McAuley Palmer (SOL 1909, SC 1910) at the Library of Congress included little for the period he was at Leavenworth, they were the most important manuscript collection I examined. The correspondence and the chapter notes for an unwritten memoir contained critiques of Leavenworth education and of the role of school-trained officers, especially on the General Staff. Palmer had studied the German General Staff and was among the first American officers to recognize the difficulties inherent in the attempt of the United States to create its own General Staff.

The papers of William T. Sherman, Elihu Root, Leonard Wood, and John J. Pershing at the Library of Congress con-

tained some useful material on the role of the army's leaders
in fostering Leavenworth education and military professionalism.

Additional information on the perspective of Leavenworth
men was made available to me by Dr. Forrest C. Pogue from
transcripts and notes on his interviews with Royden E. Beebe
(SOL 1907, SC 1908), April 6, 1961; Fay W. Brabson (SOL
1907), December 5, 1960; Charles D. Herron (SOL 1907, SC
1908), May 28, 1958; and George C. Marshall (SOL 1907, SC
1908, instructor 1908-10), April 4, 1957. Similar information
came from my own interview with Brabson, January 10, 1970,
and correspondence with Herron, March 28, 1970, Thomas B.
Catron (instructor 1912-16), March 7, 1970, and Louis M. Nuttman (SOL 1915, SC 1916), December 16, 1971.

THE LEAVENWORTH COURSE

The best information on the objectives of the course and
their content came from the annual reports and from the textbooks used. Other useful information of this sort was found
in lectures, student theses, and problems reprinted in *Cavalry
Journal, Infantry Journal,* and the *Journal of the Military
Service Institution.*

THE AEF EXPERIENCE

By far the best history of American military participation
in World War I is Edward M. Coffman, *The War to End All
Wars* (New York: Oxford University Press, 1968); the section
on organizing the AEF in the summer and fall of 1917 was
especially useful. Allan R. Millett's recent biography of General Bullard, *The General: Robert L. Bullard and Officership
in the United States Army, 1881-1925* (Westport, Conn.: Greenwood Press, 1975), includes good material on the operations of
the First Division, III Corps, and Second Army and a succinct
analysis of tactics and staff procedures in the AEF. Harvey A.

DeWeerde's *President Wilson Fights His War* (New York: Macmillan, 1968) also includes a few pertinent observations on tactics and the overall American performance.

Edward M. Coffman, "The American Military Generation Gap in World War I: The Leavenworth Clique in the A.E.F.," in William E. Geffen, ed., *Command and Commanders in Modern Warfare: Proceedings of the Second Military History Symposium, U.S. Air Force Academy* (Washington, D.C.: GPO, 1969), and the remarks on the paper by retired officers who had served in the AEF, indicate some of the problems that arose between the Leavenworth-trained staff officers and non-Leavenworth men who were often the commanders. Similarly, Senate Committee on Military Affairs, *Hearings on the Nomination of Col. Alfred W. Bjornstad, U.S. Army for Nomination to be a Brigadier General*, 68th Cong., 2d sess., 1925, provides excellent testimony by commanders, staff officers, and non-Leavenworth officers who had served as assistant staff officers as to the workings of the AEF general staffs. The role of Leavenworth graduates in key positions in the AEF has been the subject of two notable biographies: Forrest C. Pogue, *George C. Marshall: Education of a General* (New York: Viking Press, 1963), and Elliott L. Johnson, "The Military Experiences of Hugh A. Drum from 1898-1918" (Ph.D. diss., University of Wisconsin, 1975). Additional insight is provided by George C. Marshall, *Memoirs of My Services in the World War*, ed. James L. Collins, Jr. (Boston: Houghton Mifflin, 1976), a sprightly memoir written shortly after the war. Two Leavenworth men in command positions also left useful accounts of their AEF experiences: Robert Alexander, *Memoirs of World War I* (New York: Macmillan, 1931), and Charles D. Rhodes, "Diary Notes of a Soldier," unpublished manuscript, National Archives Library, chap. 8.

INDEX

American Expeditionary Forces
  general headquarters, 135-36,
    140, 145, 147-48
  general staff organization, 135-
    36
  general staff procedures, 141-49
  Leavenworth graduates in, 134-
    36, 138, 140, 142-43, 161
  schools, 136-38
  strategy, 136
  tactics, 138-40
  units
    First Army, 146-50
    I Corps, 147
    First Division, 135, 144-45
    Forty-second Division, 147
    Second Army, 143
    Seventy-eighth Division, 144
    III Corps, 143-44
    Third Division, 141
American Historical Association, 7
Andrews, Avery, 136
Applicatory method, 12-13, 15,
    39, 45-48, 64, 83-84,
    91-92

Army War College, 45, 55, 57-
    58, 112, 122, 124
Artillery School, 22, 24
Augur, Jacob A., 59

Beebe, Royden C., 77
Bell, J. Franklin, 4, 39, 59, 89,
    94, 112, 127-28
  career of, 68-69
  influence of on Leavenworth,
    69-70, 75-79
  reorganization of Leavenworth
    curriculum, 68, 70-74
  selection of Leavenworth instruc-
    tors, 73
  selection of Leavenworth stu-
    dents, 71, 77-78
Bigelow, John, 82
Bjornstad, Alfred W., 136, 143
Bliss, Tasker, 55, 57-58
Booth, Ewing E., 74
Boughton, Daniel, 127-28
Brabson, Fay, 77
Brees, Herbert J., 74

British Staff College (Camberley), 11, 13
Brown, Preston, 141
Brown, William C., 27
Buddecke, Albert, 96
    Tactical Decisions and Orders, 91
Bullard, Robert L., 77, 87, 120, 123, 143
Burnham, William P., 112

Carter, William H., 44-48, 54-59, 65
Chaffee, Adna, 55, 73
Chitty, William D., 117
Clausewitz, Carl von, 11-12
Command and General Staff College, 5
Conger, Arthur L., 89, 96-98
Cole, Edwin T., 102
Conner, Fox, 135, 147
Corbin, Henry C., 54
Craig, Malin, 147

Davidson, Howard, 117
Davis, Milton F., 78
Delbrück, Hans, 96
Dickinson, Jacob M., 123
Dickman, Joseph T., 120, 127
Dodge Commission, 54
Donnelly, Howard, 118
Drum, Hugh A., 90, 136, 146-49

Ecole supérieure de guerre, 11
Eltinge, Leroy, 90, 136
Ely, Hanson, 143-44

Field Service Regulations, 93-94, 127-28, 139
Fiske, Harold B., 90, 117, 136, 138

Fling, Frederick Morrow, 7, 98
Frederick the Great, 45

Ganoe, William A., 39
General Service and Staff College (1902-1904), 68, 70
    curriculum, 59-60, 63
    establishment of, 58-60
    impact of on the army, 65
    instruction methods, 63-65
    students, 59-62, 74
German Army, 125
    tactics, 40-41, 86-87
Grant, Ulysses, 149
Grant, Walter, 147
Griepenkerl, Otto F., 45, 141
    Studies in Applied Tactics, 90

Haight, Charles S., 74
Harbord, James G., 83, 135, 150
Hawkins, Hamilton S., 35, 38, 48
Heintzelman, Stuart, 89, 97
Henderson, G. F. R., 13
Herbst, Jürgen, 14
Herron, Charles D., 121, 135, 144
Hilyard, H. J. T., 13
Hines, John L., 143
Hubbard, Elmer, 48

Johnston, Robert M., 97

Kriegsakademie, 11-12
Kriegsspiel, 46-47

Langres Staff College, 136-38
Leach, Smith S., 60
Lee, Jesse M., 78
Lewal, Jules Louis, 11
Liggett, Hunter, 83, 120-22, 150
Logan, James A., 136
Ludlow, William, 15

McAndrew, James W., 90, 100, 136
McCleave, Robert, 147
McCook, Alexander McD., 28-29, 35, 38
Mahan, Dennis Hart, 26
"Mailing list," 121
Malone, Paul B., 136
"Manchu law," 113
Marshall, George C., 76, 83, 89, 105-06, 141, 144-45, 147, 149
Masland, John W., and Lawrence I. Radway, 5
Meuse-Argonne offensive, 139-41, 146-49
Mexican Punitive Expedition, 116
Miles, Nelson A., 53, 55
Miles, Perry L., 115
Military education, 5, 10-11, 83-84
Military professionalism, 5-7, 10-11, 120-21, 128-29
Militia instruction camps, 113-14
Miner, Charles W., 59, 69-70
Morrison, John F., 4, 121
    career of, 87-89
    influence of on U. S. Army, 89, 106
    in Russo-Japanese War, 88
    instructor at Leavenworth, 89-94, 99, 122-23
    "Morrison men," 89-90, 96
    Studies in Minor Tactics, 90
    tactical thought of, 92-94
Moseley, George Van Horn, 78, 119

Nolan, Dennis, 136

Otis, Elwell S., 24, 26

Palmer, Frederick, 149
Palmer, John M., 97, 115, 119, 125, 141
Pershing, John J., 79, 83, 114, 121, 134-36, 139-40, 146, 149
Pettit, James S., 49
Pope, John, 21, 26
Proctor, Redfield, 8
Progressive era, 8

Rhodes, Charles D., 147
Richardson, Lorrin T., 117
Root, Elihu, 4, 8, 50, 54-59, 62, 65, 69
Ruger, Thomas H., 27
Russo-Japanese War, 88

Saint-Mihiel offensive, 139-40, 146-48
Sanger, William Cary, 54
Scharnhorst, Gerhard von, 11
Schellendorff, Fritz Bronsart von, 99-100
Schofield, John M., 34-35, 48
School of Application for Infantry and Cavalry (1881-1898; redesignated Infantry and Cavalry School in 1886)
    curriculum, 24-27, 29-30, 35-36
    establishment of, 21-24
    impact of on the U. S. Army, 27, 48-50, 53, 55
    instruction methods, 25, 28-29, 35
    instructors, 25, 28
    students, 22-25, 27, 30, 35, 48-50
School of the Line (1904-1916; designated Infantry and

Cavalry School from
1904 to 1907)
curriculum, 72, 85-86, 90-94,
99, 102-07
graduates, 112-19, 124-26,
157
impact of on the U. S. Army,
75-77, 85, 104-07,
114, 117-18, 120-30
instruction methods, 75-76,
90-92, 105
instructors, 73, 89-90
organization of, 72, 74-75
students, 72, 74-75, 85, 106-
07
Scott, Hugh L., 124
Sheridan, Philip, 16, 28
Sherman, William T., 17, 22-26,
50
military education, 22-23
Staff College (1904-1916)
curriculum, 72-73, 85-86,
94-107
graduates, 112-19, 124-26,
158
impact of on the U. S. Army,
75-77, 85, 104-07, 114,
117-18, 120-30
instruction methods, 75-76,
97-98, 101, 105
instructors, 73, 89-90
organization of, 72-75
students, 72, 74-75, 85,
106-07
study of general staff duties,
99-102
study of military history,
94-99
Steele, Matthew F., 94-96
American Campaigns, 95-96
Strategy, 95

Summerall, Charles P., 121
Swift, Eben, 4, 15, 36
applicatory method, 45-48
career of, 43-45
influence of on the U. S.
Army, 45, 48
instructor at Army War College, 45
instructor at Leavenworth, 44-
48, 73, 76

Tactics, 9-10
Townsend, Edwin F., 35
"Transfer of culture," 14

U. S. Army
foreign influence on, 8-9, 13-
15, 37, 40-41, 45-47,
86-87
lyceum system, 57
military reforms, 7-9, 15-18,
34-35, 48-50, 54-59,
128-29
officer corps, 16, 31, 55-56, 78-
79, 84, 105-07, 118-20,
128-29
post schools, 57, 86, 116
schools, 21, 34-35, 55-59,
75-76
tactics, 16, 29-30, 39, 41-43,
63-64, 71, 82-85, 90-96,
115-16
Upton, Emory, 15, 17, 21-22,
54, 82

Vernois, Von Verdy du, 45, 47

Wagner, Arthur L., 4, 15, 44, 64,
71-72, 82
career of, 36-43
influence of on the U. S.

Army, 36, 38-40, 43,
48
instructor at Leavenworth, 37-
40, 45, 48
military thought of, 40-43
writings of, 36-37, 39-40
Campaign of Königgrätz,
40-41
Organization and Tactics,
42-43
*Service of Security and In-
formation,* 41-42

Walker, Kirby, 136
War College Board, 59-60, 62,
69-70
War Department General Staff,
54-56, 71-73, 83, 101,
112, 124-27, 159-60
Weigley, Russell F., 8, 39
West Point, 7, 63, 117, 121
Wood, Leonard, 76, 123-24

Young, S. B. M., 69

ABOUT THE AUTHOR

Timothy K. Nenninger is an archivist in the Military Archives
Division of the National Archives in Washington, D.C. His
articles on military topics have appeared in a variety of books
and journals.